THE
BRISTOL & BATH
COOK BOOK

A CELEBRATION OF THE AMAZING FOOD & DRINK ON OUR DOORSTEP

FOREWORD

LIVING IN THE WEST COUNTRY IS AN ABSOLUTE PRIVILEGE; THE BEAUTIFUL COUNTRYSIDE THAT SURROUNDS US EVEN IN THE CITIES IS A REASON TO BE CHEERFUL.

I started my career as a civil engineer, worked in London, and then in 2003 I lost my parents and suddenly inherited their farm. With this huge responsibility at a young age, I took the stewardship of that land very seriously. I turned it over to organic production and really wanted to share the land with others, because it's such a beautiful place as anyone who has been to Valley Fest or The Community Farm will testify.

I knew instinctively that farming in a way which enhanced the environment was the right thing to do, and as a result it produced some of the best-tasting beef in the world. The farm enabled other visions to also be realised; setting up The Story Butchers and subsequently Meatbox has enabled us to really shout about our ethical meat supply. Co-founding and opening the gates to The Community Farm fills me with enormous pride about what the future could hold for many other like-minded land owners.

I have always dreamed of having a restaurant on the farm, and while we haven't quite achieved that yet, our restaurants – Root and Yurt Lush – champion the very best local and seasonal ingredients along with our own fresh, free-range, native and organic meats. We are blessed with some of the finest chefs who have designed some of the most memorable meals I have ever tasted.

However, we have succeeded in running a festival for the last six years! Valley Fest, which we like to call the best-tasting music festival in the south west, showcases what we have on offer in the region. As well as big headliners, we're using that platform to educate people about the importance of climate-friendly and local food. Food, feasting and markets are all part of the fun. My parents were big party lovers and would have liked nothing better than to host a decent festival overlooking the lake.

Here on the farm we're busy improving soil health, creating renewable food systems and going carbon neutral. All of these things will become more evident in our daily lives and I hope to see a massive change in how our restaurants and cafés can help shape the future. Bristol and Bath are well and truly top foodie destinations and I am proud to be a part of that map.

Luke Hasell

CONTENTS

The Bristol & Bath Cook Book

©2019 Meze Publishing Ltd. All rights reserved.

First edition printed in 2019 in the UK.

ISBN: 9781910863558

Thank you: Luke Hasell

Compiled by: Anna Tebble

Written by: Katie Fisher

Photography by: Matt Crowder
(www.mattcrowder.co.uk)

Additional photography: Jake Morley
(www.jakemorley.co.uk)

Edited by: Phil Turner, Chris Brierley

Designed by: Paul Cocker

Contributors: Rupinder Casimir, Lydia Fitzsimons,
Michael Johnson, Sarah Koriba, Marek Nowicki

Cover art: David Broadbent
(www.davidbroadbent.co.uk)

me:ze
PUBLISHING

Published by Meze Publishing Limited

Unit 1b, 2 Kelham Square

Kelham Riverside

Sheffield S3 8SD

Web: www.mezepublishing.co.uk

Telephone: 0114 275 7709

Email: info@mezepublishing.co.uk

Printed in Great Britain by Bell and Bain Ltd, Glasgow

TAKE A BOW

BRISTOL OLD VIC HAS UNDERGONE A HUGE RENOVATION AND 1766 BAR & KITCHEN PROVIDES THE PERFECT SETTING TO SOAK UP THE CONTEMPORARY ARCHITECTURE OF ITS IMPRESSIVE NEW FOYER.

1766 Bar & Kitchen is a collaboration between well-known local company Fosters Events and Bristol Old Vic, the oldest continuously working theatre in the English-speaking world. The centrepiece of the new foyer is the original 250 year old theatre's façade, revealed to the public for the first time, which provides a spectacular backdrop to the new restaurant space.

Open since September 2018, 1766 Bar & Kitchen serves food and drink from morning through till evening. Start the day with homemade granola or fried halloumi, enjoy a choice of salads over lunch, choose from an à la carte menu of small plates or three courses before a show, and grab a cocktail at the bar. The concept has always been to embrace the nature of the building as a working theatre, and for the menu to be inspired by the same creativity. Movement in the space naturally ebbs and flows with the performances and a welcoming atmosphere with local, seasonal menus are at the heart of the '1766' ethos.

During the day, many writers use the spacious foyer in which 1766 Bar & Kitchen is set as an inspirational place to work or people-watch, while in the evening the dramatic character of the space creates a much more intimate atmosphere for evening diners. Fosters Events' Tom Green has championed head chef Coco Barone's Italian roots. She focuses on using quality seasonal produce, prepared simply, so the ingredients can really take centre stage. The epic Sunday Roast she serves up has already gained a big following across the city.

"In Italy, mealtimes are about bringing people together around the table to share the food and their day. I focus on the main ingredient in a dish, put it in the limelight and showcase its true flavours with an occasional playful twist," she says. Tom describes the approach as "food people really want to eat," and is proud to have talented people at the helm of this destination, including local Front of House legend, Barbara 'Babs' Wragg.

1766 Bar & Kitchen has already been nominated for both a Crumbs Award and a Bristol Life Award, so the emphasis for everyone is on "not losing sight of where we started, and keeping this beautiful place on a high" as Bristol Old Vic moves into another phase of its long and incredible life.

Photo: Harrison Dowling Media

Photo: Harrison Dowling Media

Photo: Evoke Pictures Lifestyle

Photo: Evoke Pictures Lifestyle

1766
BAR & KITCHEN

SET THE SCENE

COFFEE

Single origin beans from Chiltern Coffee

Espresso   £1.80 / £2.00
Americano   £2.00 / £2.30
Cortado   £2.00 / £2.50
Flat white   £2.40
Cappuccino   £2.60
Latte   £2.60
Mocha   £2.70
Cappuccino   £3.00
Hot chocolate   £2.80
Kids hot choc   70p
Marshmallows   £1.20
Syrup or switch to oat or almond milk   40p
                                              30p

TEA

Canton loose leaf teas
English breakfast, Earl grey, Roiboos, Oolong,   £2.20
Green, Assam, Darjeeling, Peppermint, Chamomile

Bring your own, reusable cup for 30p off take away hot drinks.

Photo: Harrison Dowling Media

Photo: Evoke Pictures Lifestyle

GARGANELLI PASTA

This is a classic pasta dish from the Emilia-Romagna area in Northern Italy that works well with numerous sauces, including meat ragu such as bolognese. To make this as authentic as possible, you will need to use a garganelli/gnocchi board with a wooden paddle which creates the distinctive ridges.

FOR THE PASTA

330g semolina flour

5g fine salt

80g egg yolk

30ml water

Flour, for dusting

FOR THE PANGRATTATO

1 clove of garlic, minced

Splash of olive oil

40g breadcrumbs

1 lemon, zested

FOR THE SAUCE

30g white onion, finely chopped

100g extra-virgin olive oil

2 cloves of garlic, minced

200g tenderstem broccoli, blanched

50g white wine

200g sun-dried tomato, chopped

40g capers, roughly chopped

1 fresh red chilli, finely chopped

½ bunch of parsley, picked and coarsely chopped

40g Parmesan, grated

FOR THE PASTA

Sift the semolina flour and salt into a mixing bowl. Add the egg yolk then slowly add the water while stirring. If you are using an electric mixer, be careful not to over work the dough. Once it comes together, cover and leave to rest in the fridge for at least 1 hour.

Using a pasta machine, fold the chilled dough repeatedly until the sheets are smooth to the touch and approximately 1cm thick. Cut the pasta into 5cm squares. Make sure you let them dry for a few minutes at this stage, otherwise the pasta will flatten out after shaping.

Lightly flour the garganelli/gnocchi board and place one of the squares on it with a point facing you so it looks like a diamond. Roll the square around the dowel from the bottom to the top of the diamond, pressing down lightly on the dough as you roll. Press down to seal the ends of the roll together. Place the garganelli in a tray and sprinkle with flour to avoid them sticking together. You can make these with an ordinary chopping board and round chopstick if needed.

FOR THE PANGRATTATO

On a low heat, fry the minced garlic with olive oil until golden brown. Add the breadcrumbs and fry until they are lightly coloured and the oil has been absorbed. Take the pan off the heat and stir the lemon zest through, mixing well.

FOR THE SAUCE

Bring a pan of salted water to the boil for the pasta. Meanwhile, fry the diced onion in the oil until lightly soft and translucent, and then add the garlic and cook for a couple of minutes. Add the blanched broccoli and cook for 1 minute over a medium heat. Pour in the white wine and let it evaporate over a high heat. Add the sun-dried tomato, capers and chilli.

Cook the pasta for at least 3 minutes in the boiling water, adding a small ladle of boiling water to the sauce as you do. Strain the pasta and toss it in the sauce until you reach a happy consistency (the sauce needs to coat the pasta). Stir through the chopped parsley.

TO SERVE

Place the pasta carefully in a warmed deep bowl and scatter Parmesan and pangrattato over the top. Buon appetito!

Photo: Matt Crowder

Preparation time: 30 minutes, plus 1 hour chilling | Cooking time: approx. 20 minutes | Serves: 4

GET A
GOOD
GUT FEELING

BATH CULTURE HOUSE FOUNDER LUCIE IS PASSIONATE ABOUT SHARING HER
NATURALLY FERMENTED FOODS AND KNOWLEDGE OF GOOD GUT HEALTH.

Lucie is a trained biologist and a food lover, so it's not altogether surprising that her two passions have come together in the shape of Bath Culture House. She began the venture in May 2016 while working as a cheesemaker, but swapped dairy for plants to explore the wonderful world of fermentation. As a self-confessed microbe and gut health geek, Lucie wanted to create vegan, gluten-free and 'tummy-loving' food and drink by going back to basics and using clean ingredients.

The results are four handmade products, beautifully designed in plastic-free packaging. Her sauerkraut comes in two varieties: with Cornish seaweed or turmeric, ginger and apple. There is an aromatic live kimchi, which also comes in a ketchup, and several flavours of kombucha including hibiscus and jasmine flower. Five types of vegan 'cheese' complete the current line-up: garlic and herb, sumac and cumin, turmeric and black pepper, activated charcoal and smoked chipotle chilli. Bath Culture House uses organic ingredients wherever possible, including all the cashew nuts and almonds used in the 'cheese' making process, and works with local suppliers for sourcing.

Being part of and contributing to a community is very important to Lucie, whether that involves sticking with regional retailers instead of pursuing supermarket stockists, or passing on her craft by teaching at Demuths Cookery School, where she runs a fermentation workshop. Her business began life in Bath – hence the name – but production soon moved to a unit in the Somerset countryside, nestled among the Mendips between the two cities where most products are currently sold.

The plan is to continue expanding, however, and cross counties to reach people further afield via wholefoods and independents. The website is a one-stop shop for all the products, and has also partnered with Bristol-based eco-friendly delivery service, Good Sixty. You can also find Bath Culture House goodies in Bristol's Scoop Wholefoods (where kombucha refills are sold from kegs) and Bath's The Grapes, as well as cafés, restaurants, local markets and even a cheesemongers.

Lucie is committed to working with her stockists directly because connecting with people is part of Bath Culture House's ethos; it's not just about great tasting food and drink, but about promoting good health and inspiring others to eat well too. She hopes to take on some members of staff in the near future, who will help her continue making and packing everything that the company produces, because knowing where your food comes from is as important for the gut as it is for the taste buds!

KIMCHI PANCAKES

Korean mung bean pancakes are also known as bindae-tteok. These delicious pancakes are made from mung beans and flavoured with kimchi. This recipe is from Demuths Cookery School, Bath, where I teach Fermentation. I'm often asked 'how do you eat kimchi?' so I chose this recipe to inspire kimchi lovers.

150g mung beans, soaked in plenty of cold water for 12 hours

75-100ml cold water

1 tsp toasted sesame oil

60g beansprouts, chopped

125g kimchi, chopped

2 tbsp kimchi liquid from the jar

3 spring onions, finely chopped

½ tsp Korean chilli flakes (gochugaru)

2 cloves of garlic, minced

2 tsp soy sauce or tamari (gluten-free)

¼ tsp salt

1-2 tbsp glutinous rice flour or cornflour

Sunflower oil, for frying

FOR THE DIPPING SAUCE

1 tbsp soy sauce or tamari (gluten-free)

1 tsp rice vinegar

Pinch of Korean chilli flakes (gochugaru)

Drain and rinse the mung beans, then purée them in a food processor with 75ml of water until as smooth as possible. It should be a very thick, porridge-like batter, so add a little more water if the mixture isn't puréeing sufficiently.

Transfer the purée to a bowl and stir in the sesame oil, beansprouts, kimchi, kimchi liquid, spring onions, garlic, soy sauce or tamari, Korean chilli flakes and salt. Add enough rice flour or cornflour to combine everything so there is no visible separation of liquid in the batter. Taste and adjust the seasoning to suit, adding more soy sauce, tamari or chilli if necessary.

Heat two tablespoons of oil in a frying pan (preferably non-stick) and drop in three separate tablespoons of batter at a time, spacing them well apart to allow for spreading. Flip them over carefully after a minute or two. They need to be golden brown on both sides and firm when pressed to ensure they are cooked through. Place onto a tray lined with kitchen towel to absorb excess oil, and keep warm in a low oven while you cooking the remaining pancakes.

FOR THE DIPPING SAUCE

Stir the soy sauce or tamari and rice vinegar together in a small bowl with the chilli flakes. Serve this alongside the warm bindae-tteok. Enjoy!

Preparation time: 12 hours | Cooking time: 5 minutes | Serves: 12

CREAM OF THE CROP

ARTISAN, AWARD-WINNING ORGANIC CHEESE IS MADE BY HAND AT PARK FARM NEAR BATH, USING ORGANIC MILK FROM GRASS-FED COWS AND DRAWING ON A MULTI-GENERATIONAL FAMILY HERITAGE.

There's an old farming saying – 'look after your cows and your cows will look after you' – which speaks to the heart of what happens at Park Farm where The Bath Soft Cheese Company is based. The Padfield family, whose fourth generation, Hugh, is the farm's current owner, take a traditional approach to raising and grazing their small herd of 160, mainly Holstein Friesian cows and to their artisan, handmade cheese.

In the 1990s, Hugh's father, Graham, tracked down an original recipe for Bath Cheese in an old grocer's book, which stipulated that the cheese must be made with full cream milk, that salt be sprinkled on the young cheeses using a feather, and that the cheese was soft and covered with white mould. Whilst they don't use feathers in today's cheesemaking, the team at Park Farm use the same traditional artisan methods which gives the cheeses more flavour and an unbeatably creamy texture.

The range has had more than its fair share of awards. During 2019, Bath Soft Cheese was named Supreme Champion at the Artisan Cheese Awards, while the Wyfe of Bath cheese won Supreme Champion at the UK's biggest international cheese awards; first out of over 5,000 cheeses. The Bath Blue was developed in 2010 and was crowned World Champion Cheese at the 2014 World Cheese Awards. The latest addition to the range, the Merry Wyfe, is a cider-washed version of the Wyfe of Bath, using cider made with apples from the farm's orchards. It's already won a few awards; hopefully it too will be a supreme champion soon.

All of the cheeses at Bath Soft Cheese Company are made using organic milk from Park Farm's own herd. The grass-fed cows produce rich creamy milk that is crucial to the quality of the cheese. The milk for making cheese is taken just as the morning milking finishes; you can't get fresher than that.

The café and shop at Park Farm allow all their customers to visit the farm and better understand the local provenance of the cheese. As well as a deli counter offering samples of all the cheeses, there are viewing galleries for both the cheese dairy and milking parlour. The public can munch on cheese toasties and drink milkshakes while watching the cows being milked or the cheese being made. All the ingredients used in the café are either from the farm or from a host of local suppliers.

BATH SOFT MAC 'N' CHEESE

This dish started as a special but has now become a staple in the café. The sauce features two of our award winning cheeses (both crowned 2019 Supreme Champions): Wyfe of Bath and Bath Soft Cheese, making it rich, earthy and distinctive. Using our pasteurised unhomogenised organic milk, it creates an intensely creamy consistency, contributing to the overall depth and flavour of the dish.

300g macaroni

45g butter

45g plain flour

600ml Park Farm organic milk

200g Wyfe of Bath, grated

1 Bath Soft Cheese, halved and broken up into small pieces

1 tbsp finely chopped fresh parsley

60g breadcrumbs

Salt and freshly ground black pepper

FOR THE EASY GARLIC BREAD

45g butter, at room temperature

1 clove of garlic, finely chopped

1 tsp finely chopped fresh parsley

8 slices of local sourdough

Preheat the oven to 180°c.

Bring a large pan of salted water to the boil and add the macaroni. Cook for 5 minutes then drain (the pasta shouldn't be fully cooked through at this point).

Meanwhile, melt the butter in a saucepan over a low heat. When the butter is fully melted, add the flour and stir continuously for 2 minutes. Add the milk a little at a time, still stirring continuously. When all the milk has been incorporated, gently cook the sauce for 5 minutes, stirring all the time until it has thickened.

Remove the pan from the heat and add 150g of the grated Wyfe of Bath and all the Bath Soft cheese, stirring them into the sauce until evenly distributed and beginning to melt. Taste the sauce then season it with salt and pepper.

Add the drained pasta to the sauce, stir to combine and then pour the mixture into an ovenproof dish. Mix together the remaining grated Wyfe of Bath, the breadcrumbs and finely chopped parsley. Sprinkle this evenly on top. Bake for 25 minutes in the preheated oven until golden brown.

While the macaroni cheese is baking, make the easy garlic bread to serve with it. Combine the butter, chopped garlic and finely chopped parsley then spread evenly over the slices of sourdough. Put them in the oven for the remaining 3 to 5 minutes of the macaroni cheese's cooking time.

Plate the macaroni cheese and serve with a couple of garlic bread slices per person.

Preparation time: 30 minutes | Cooking time: 25 minutes | Serves: 4

TWO'S COMPANY

THIS LOCAL INDEPENDENT BAR AND RESTAURANT HAS A BEAUTIFULLY REALISED CONCEPTUAL APPROACH TO FOOD AND DRINK, LOCATED IN THE HEART OF BRISTOL WITH A SISTER RESTAURANT AT WAPPING WHARF.

Brace & Browns has been welcoming diners in the heart of Bristol for almost ten years. The independent bar and restaurant is still owned by David Brown, who created the concept, and is a much-loved gem amidst the city's food and drink scene. Emphasis is placed on creating a warm and friendly atmosphere for guests to enjoy a British take on tapas during the week, or indulge in Saturday brunches and Sunday lunches over the weekend. The bar is always open for your favourite tipple, best enjoyed on the decked terrace during sunny afternoons, or whenever takes your fancy!

Head chef Andrew Myatt brings the menu of small plates to life with his kitchen team, creating seasonally-inspired dishes with locally sourced produce that embrace flavours from around the world to give each one an exciting twist. "We like to support businesses, residents, and produce in the area as much as we can, alongside finding the best ingredients for our customers," says general manager Josh. Each item is carefully thought out and balanced, with plenty of vegetarian, vegan and gluten-free options that are part of the whole concept rather than an added extra.

Bar and restaurant merge on the upper floor, encouraging a relaxed and casual feel no matter where you want to eat or drink. The wide range of cocktails, spirits, draught beers and wine covers all the bases: not forgetting prosecco for those weekend get-togethers over good food, fun and friends! This approach to creating destinations people want to return to has been brought to life a second time at Harbour & Browns, the smaller sister restaurant of Brace & Browns. It takes the same concepts and downsizes them to fit within the modern, stylish shipping containers on Wapping Wharf (hence the name) which offers light-filled spaces and views too good to miss.

Diners at Harbour & Browns can see the chefs preparing food from their tables, adding to the experience alongside its own distinct character and menus. Both restaurants can host parties, weddings, functions and other private events year-round. The entire space can be hired at Harbour & Browns, while Brace & Browns has a private dining room downstairs. "People love coming back here; that rare combination of new faces and customers returning year after year tells us we're doing something right," says Josh, "so we hope to continue building on that reputation and keep both venues the best they can be."

SEARED VENISON LOIN WITH TRUFFLE MASH, SPRING GREENS & BLACKBERRY RED WINE SAUCE

*Game goes really well with blackberries, as their sharpness cuts through the rich
lean meat. The addition of truffle mash and fresh spring greens make this a lovely
indulgent autumnal dinner.*

500g Maris Piper potatoes

1 tbsp salt

500ml beef stock

250ml red wine

2 tbsp tomato paste

2 cloves of garlic

1 head of spring greens

1 tbsp vegetable oil

2 venison steaks

Salt and black pepper

20ml truffle oil

40g butter

1 punnet of blackberries

Peel and chop the potatoes, put them into a pan with enough cold water to cover
them and add the salt. Place over a medium heat to simmer.

While the potatoes are cooking, put the beef stock, red wine, tomato paste and
garlic in another saucepan over a medium heat. Whisk everything together and
start to reduce the liquid. The sauce is ready when it has reduced to a quarter of its
original volume.

To prepare the spring greens, take the root off, layer the leaves evenly on top of
each other then cut out the stalk in one go. Tightly roll up the leaves lengthways and
then finely slice.

Heat up a heavy-based frying pan and add the vegetable oil. Season the venison
steaks well with salt and pepper. Once the pan is hot, add the venison steaks
and sear on one side for about 2 minutes then turn over and repeat for about 6
minutes. This will make the steaks medium-rare, so cook longer if you prefer them
well done.

Once the steaks are nearly ready, transfer them to a plate to rest. This will relax the
meat and make it more tender as the juices can be absorbed.

When the potatoes are ready, turn off the heat, drain, then put them back into the
pan. Add the truffle oil and about 40g of butter. Mash until smooth and adjust the
seasoning to taste.

Drop the spring greens into a pan of boiling water and simmer for about 3 minutes
until cooked, then drain and season with salt and pepper.

Take the garlic out of the red wine sauce and add the blackberries. After a minute
or two, when the blackberries have softened, take off the heat and decant into a jug
for serving. Plate the steaks, mash and spring greens then enjoy.

Preparation time: 15 minutes | Cooking time: approx. 20 minutes | Serves: 2

THE ROUTE TO
FOODIE
HEAVEN

HIDDEN GEMS, DELICIOUS DISHES AND REAL FOOD EXPERIENCES ARE THE ORDER OF THE DAY FOR THE BRISTOL FOOD TOUR, A COMPANY SET UP BY FOOD LOVERS *FOR* FOOD LOVERS THAT LEAVES NO STONE UNTURNED ACROSS THE CULINARY LANDSCAPE OF THE CITY.

Why weren't great food tours happening in the UK? This was the question that Alice and Jo asked themselves on returning to Bristol – the wonderful city they both moved to for university and now call home – after experiencing food tours while on travels abroad. At that point they had been independently mulling over the idea of setting up something similar in their city, so when Alice mentioned the idea to Jo, they decided to collaborate 'in true Bristol style'. And so, the Bristol Food Tour was established in August 2016, with the aim of showcasing the foodie gems that abounded in Stokes Croft initially, as it was their foodie stomping ground.

That first tour took guests on a walk via eight independent eateries for tasty samples along with fun-size bites of cultural and social history. Instagram became a great way to reach other foodies and grow the business steadily with weekend tours, but when articles were published about their venture in magazines such as Crumbs, Bristol 24/7 and Bristol Life, Alice and Jo found their tours sold out for the next few months. It was a big turnaround, and helped tBFT to expand not only with more bookings, but more independents who approached them, keen to be involved.

As things got busier, people who came on the tours offered to help out, and two eventually turned into an all-female team of tour guides and a fabulous social media manager. All of the guides have different backgrounds, interests and styles, so Alice and Jo encourage them to bring what they're passionate about to the group, ensuring each individual tour has personality and real insight.

tBFT now operates three distinct tours in different parts of the city: Stokes Croft, South of the River, and East to West, as well as 'The Great Bristol Food Tour', a collaboration with Cycle the City which – as you might expect – is done by bicycle. They also do one-off special event tours that might focus on a particular neighbourhood or type of food where exciting new businesses are springing up, and if proving popular these can become new additions to the regular line up. "Our core theme is really just independents with a great story and delicious food," says Alice. "We initially drew up a massive list of places that we'd like to visit and went from there, so there's real variety."

They also organise private, bespoke and corporate tours for anyone who loves food and wants to celebrate an occasion by visiting a hand-picked selection of Bristol's culinary hotspots. These tailored routes can even be made vegan, or as luxurious as you like; having built up a vast network of contacts in the food world, Alice and Jo are perfectly placed to curate something really special.

Whether you have lived in Bristol for years or you've only just arrived, the idea behind their business is to introduce people to what tBFT believes are the best places across the city that could be newly opened, old favourites, hidden gems, diamonds in the rough or simply not shouted about enough. Alice and Jo have the tough job of eating out in Bristol a lot, purely for research purposes, of course. They also get recommendations from tour guests, social media, and the dedicated members of their team who go out of their way to discover yet more eateries that are too good to miss.

Being part of a tour means plenty of publicity, which is great for small businesses, and the owners or chefs who put so much passion and hard work into what they do are brought into the limelight. "We want to encourage people to go back for more!" says Jo. This gives people the rare opportunity to connect with the food they eat via those who create it. "We love sharing their stories; that's what it's all about for us," says Jo.

In 2018 the Bristol Food Tour won Best Food Event from Foozie Bristol, and were shortlisted for Best Food Event by Crumbs in 2019. After gaining attention and developing their home-grown business so successfully in just a few years, Alice and Jo are proud of what they've achieved, but not pushing to expand further. Keeping things small means retaining the fantastic quality that sets their tours apart. Groups are always a maximum of about eight people and the majority of tours run on Saturdays as both women – and most of their guides – still work full-time in other jobs, though bespoke tours can take place during the week.

The atmosphere of the tours is as important as the routes they follow and the businesses they take people to. They want everyone to feel like they're amongst friends, sharing food, hearing stories, and generally having a lovely laid-back experience. Bringing people together through food is the Bristol Food Tour's raison d'être, and it's doing wonders for the smörgåsbord of independent eateries thriving in Bristol.

A FLIPPING
GOOD
TIME

BURGER THEORY TRANSFORMS THE FAST FOOD FAVOURITE INTO SOMETHING CREATIVE AND REFINED AT THE BUZZING BRISTOL RESTAURANT ON ST STEPHEN STREET.

Rory Perriment and Nick Makin are the 'creative burger people' behind Burger Theory. The co-owners and friends set themselves apart from the rest when it comes to stacking the perfect patty, thanks to their commitment to creativity and passion for finding culinary inspiration in all corners of the globe. The Bristol-based restaurant focuses solely on burgers because they love that they're essentially a whole meal in a bun. "There are so many flavours out in the world, and we wanted to make the most of them," Rory says.

The story of Burger Theory started in 2012, but it was August 2017 that heralded the first proper premises opening in Bristol. Before then, owner and founder Rory Perriment ran residencies and pop ups, but taking on the lease of a former restaurant allowed him and head chef Nick Makin to do things their own way. This is evident in the eclectic and inclusive menu of burgers, cocktails, dirty fries, craft beers and epic milkshakes.

Diners can expect balanced and well-thought out flavour combinations and beautiful presentation in a casual burger style that makes you want to tuck straight in rather than taking a picture, although they are perfect for Instagram foodies!

From Korean fried chicken with sticky chilli glaze to a tofu and quinoa patty topped with smoked cheddar and halloumi, Burger Theory takes you on an international tasting trip.

In contrast to this global outlook, the ingredients are sourced much closer to home with an emphasis on top quality produce. The buns are sourced from a local bakery and all the meat used at the restaurant is supplied by Walter Rose Butchers which is renowned as one of the best catering butchers in the country, championed by chefs such as Tom Kerridge and Glyn Purnell. Beef patties can be traced back to a single farm, all chicken is free-range and all the accompanying sauces and pickles are made in-house.

Before it became a restaurant, Burger Theory was known to a more select fan base from years of mobile flipping and stacking at music festivals across the south west. You can still find the catering side of the venture at Love Saves The Day, Tokyo World, The Downs and many more. Whether you're a Bristolian or a festival-goer, carnivore or vegan, family or friends, Burger Theory has the uniquely creative answer to all your burger needs.

BACON AND ALE JAM BURGERS

Whether in a burger or on a slice of hot sourdough toast, our bacon jam is perfect comfort food. Inspired by our affiliation with Bristol brewers Moor Beer Company, this recipe is made with Old Freddy Walker, which is an ale so dark it almost tastes like coffee.

FOR THE BACON JAM

700g streaky bacon, cut into 1cm pieces

2 medium onions, finely diced

1 tbsp garlic purée

125ml cider vinegar

100g dark brown sugar

70ml maple syrup

560ml Moor Beer's Old Freddy Walker, or other dark ale (alternatively you can use a cup of strong black coffee)

FOR THE BEER BATTERED GHERKINS

3 large gherkins

8g yeast

½ tsp sugar

200ml beer (we used Moor Beer's Nor'Hop)

140g plain flour

½ tsp salt

FOR THE BURGERS

1kg 20-25% fat beef mince

6 slices of Swiss cheese

Sea salt and black pepper

IN THE BUN

6 burger buns of your choice

Mayo

Lettuce

Tomato, sliced

Red onion, thinly sliced

Dijon mustard

FOR THE BACON JAM

Cook the streaky bacon in a saucepan until the fat is rendered and the bacon is lightly browned. Remove the bacon and discard all but three tablespoons of the fat. Soften the onions and garlic on a medium heat in the fat until translucent. Add the vinegar, brown sugar, maple syrup and beer then bring to the boil. Add the bacon and stir to combine. Simmer on a low heat until most of the liquid has evaporated and what's left looks syrupy. Transfer the hot jam to a sterilised jar. Store for up to one month in the fridge (not that it will last that long!)

FOR THE BEER BATTERED GHERKINS

Prepare the batter at least 1 hour in advance. Combine the beer with the yeast and sugar, then sift in the flour and add the salt. Whisk everything together until you have a smooth batter.

To cook, heat a pan of oil or a deep fat fryer up to 165°c. Slice the gherkins into quarters lengthways and toss in a little flour. Dip the gherkins in the batter and drop into the oil. Fry until crisp.

FOR THE BURGERS

Divide the beef into six equal balls. Place each ball between two pieces of baking parchment. Press down with the bottom of a plate until the patty is the right thickness.

Bring a frying pan up to a medium high heat. The beef should sizzle when it hits the pan. Just before you put the beef patties in the pan, season them to taste with sea salt and black pepper. Fry the beef patties on one side for 2 minutes then flip them over. Put a scoop of bacon jam and a slice of Swiss cheese on top, then put a lid on the pan. Leave for 2 minutes so the cheese melts, then transfer the burgers onto a warm plate to rest for 30 seconds.

Meanwhile, toast the buns and then dress the base of each one with mayo, lettuce, onion and tomato. When the patties are ready, stack your burger. Place the beef with bacon jam and melted cheese on the dressed bun, then add the fried gherkins, drizzle over some Dijon mustard and finish with the bun tops.

We call this 'the moor burger' at the restaurant because it's made with Moor Beer, but also because you just can't help but go back for more!

Preparation time: 30 minutes | Cooking time: 2 hours | Serves: 6 (plus extra bacon jam)

THE
GOOD
LIFE

CASTLE FARM MIDFORD IS ALL ABOUT GOOD FOOD, FROM PRODUCE GROWN IN THE ORGANIC GARDEN TO THEMED MONTHLY SUPPER CLUBS ALONGSIDE THE RESTAURANT, ALL RUN BY A VERY ENTERPRISING COUPLE.

When Leah and Pravin met, they were working together in Spain as front of house and chef respectively. The industry that drew them together did end up keeping them apart when it came to working hours though, and having moved back to the UK, married, and had children, they wanted to make a change that would create better lifestyles for them both. Producing a sell-out supper club at Castle Farm Midford, owned by Mark and Jo Edwards, led to the couple enquiring about leasing the venue full time. "They said yes and we just went for it," remembers Leah.

In June 2018 the restaurant and shop got a lick of paint and opened to the public. Pravin's experience as a head chef combined with his Asian and Scandinavian heritage brought new life to the menus, making the most of owner Jo's organic garden which they plan to take on themselves in 2020. The aim is to source ingredients as sustainably as possible while making space to explore food creatively. Friday evenings are all about Asian cuisine for example, which is a real passion of Pravin's, and Leah dreams up intricate and thoughtful themes for their monthly Saturday supper clubs, which might celebrate local foraging or transport guests to the Middle East for an evening.

On Sundays traditional roasts are the star of the show, served on sharing platters with a bit of everything for tucking into. The breakfast and lunch dishes change on a weekly basis, which keeps staff, chefs and guests alike engaged in the flexible and evolving business. "It's really about trying new things and having fun," says Leah, "and part of that is appealing to our team's individual interests and making sure they are genuinely happy to work with us here." The team is small but have nearly all worked with Leah and Pravin before, so there's a lot of understanding between them.

Despite not yet standing still, Leah and Pravin have big plans for the future which include developing the shop to make more garden produce available to buy, as well as incorporating it more extensively into the menus. There's potential workshop space for creatives to share Castle Farm Midford, they are hopeful the regular cookery classes will make a return too, and bespoke events and weddings add yet another string to the bow. Above all, Leah and Pravin are driven by their interests, talents and vision for a foodie idyll that feeds you well in every sense of the word.

CASTLE
FARM

Organic Farm / Restaurant
Café / Shop

SEASONAL CORDIALS
* ROSEHIP
* LEMON & THYME
* ELDERBERRY

RED LENTIL DHAL WITH MALAYSIAN ROTI

This is a firm favourite at Castle Farm and one of the few dishes never taken off the ever-changing lunch menu due to its popularity. Classic Indian dhal is the ultimate comfort food: warm and spicy, full of nutrition and best served with fluffy basmati rice or simply mopped up with a golden, flaky roti. These two dishes represent chef Pravin's Indian and Malaysian heritage in one tasty combo.

FOR THE CURRY

50ml rapeseed oil

½ tsp mustard seeds

½ tsp cumin seeds

2 tbsp diced onions

2 tsp chopped garlic

1 tsp curry leaf

½ a red chilli, sliced

1 tsp turmeric powder

1 tsp cumin powder

300ml red lentils

Salt, to taste

Lemon juice, to taste

FOR THE ROTI

360g plain flour

240ml lukewarm water

1 egg

2 tsp salt

1 tsp sugar

1 tsp condensed milk

FOR THE CURRY

Heat the rapeseed oil in a saucepan on a low heat and add the mustard and cumin seeds. After a minute add the onions and sweat them gently. Add the garlic, curry leaf and chilli and cook for another couple of minutes. Add the dry spices and red lentils, then cover with water. Allow to simmer for about 20 to 30 minutes, or until the lentils are soft and the dhal has become thick and creamy. You might have to adjust the amount of water, adding a little more or cooking the dhal for a little longer to get the right consistency. Check the seasoning, add a squeeze of lemon and adjust the spicing to your taste.

FOR THE ROTI

Mix all the ingredients in a bowl until they come together, then turn the dough onto the work surface. Knead by hand for 5 to 10 minutes until the dough is smooth and elastic. Cover with a little oil and cling film. Leave in the fridge for 12 to 24 hours for the dough to rest.

Once rested, divide the dough into six even balls, place them on a tray and oil the top of the dough balls slightly. Allow to rest for another 12 to 24 hours in the fridge.

While the dhal is cooking, remove the dough balls from the fridge and place them onto a lightly oiled work surface. Press the dough down as much as you can until the balls are flat. Roll the dough out as thinly as possible with a rolling pin, or ideally toss the flattened dough in a circular motion.

Once the roti are wafer thin, fold them into a square shape and fry them in an oiled pan until golden brown. Serve with the dhal.

Preparation time: 15 minutes, plus 2-4 days for the roti | Cooking time: approx. 1 hour | Serves: 6-8

SWEDISH CINNAMON BUNS

Being born and raised in Stockholm, Pravin was brought up baking these buns which are so synonymous with Scandinavia. Baked fresh daily at Castle Farm, served golden brown, soft and fluffy, and full of sticky, sweet cinnamon, these delights never last long. Best served with a hot cup of coffee.

FOR THE DOUGH

50g yeast

500ml milk, warmed to 37°c

150g butter, melted and slightly cooled

450g plain flour

450g strong bread flour

100g sugar

1 egg, beaten

2 tsp freshly ground cardamom

1 tsp salt

FOR THE FILLING

200g soft butter

3 tsp ground cinnamon

200g soft light brown sugar

1 egg beaten

Pearl sugar, for sprinkling

Golden syrup, to drizzle

To make the dough, dissolve the yeast in the warm milk then pour into a bowl or kitchen mixer. Add the remaining ingredients and work the dough for 10 minutes until smooth and elastic. Cover the dough with a towel and allow it to prove in a warm place for 40 to 60 minutes until doubled in size.

In the meantime, combine the soft butter, cinnamon and sugar into a paste to create your filling. Once the dough is sufficiently proved, place it on a lightly floured work surface. Roll the dough into a rectangular shape about 1.5cm thick. Spread the cinnamon paste evenly over the dough.

Divide the dough into three strips, fold the bottom piece over and then do the same with the top piece, so you are left with one thick rectangular piece with three layers. Cut the dough into equal strips of approximately finger width. Take each strip of dough, twist gently and roll it into a swirl.

Place on a baking tray and allow the buns to prove for 40 minutes. Preheat the oven to 200°c while you brush the proved buns with the beaten egg and sprinkle on the pearl sugar. Bake them in the preheated oven for 10 to 12 minutes. Once golden, remove the cinnamon buns from the oven and drizzle with golden syrup. Serve warm.

Preparation time: approx. 1 hour | Baking time: 10-12 minutes | Makes: 30-36 buns

UNRAVELLING THE
MYSTERIES OF CHOCOLATE

TUCKED AWAY IN A PICTURESQUE COURTYARD IN CONGRESBURY STANDS A
CONVERTED BARN THAT HOUSES A CHOCOLATE LOVERS' HEAVEN...

The Chocolate Tart is a place to come together or come alone, and learn how to make, taste and enjoy one of the country's favourite treats. Based in Congresbury, this chocolate school is run from a specialised kitchen amidst beautiful surroundings, which include B&B accommodation for those travelling from afar. From tempering to tasting, the many workshops run by The Chocolate Tart teach people new skills and result in impressive creations to take home, but most importantly they are wall to wall fun for anyone who is fascinated by chocolate!

A background in high-end event catering gave Lisa the expertise to become a teacher and business owner, but it was creating a dessert for the Queen that inspired her to dedicate that talent to chocolate. Creating an edible cup in which to serve a neater version of Her Majesty's favourite treat, Eton Mess was the beginning of that journey, and Lisa went on to expand her first one hour workshop into the range of hands-on experiences she offers today.

From bespoke one-to-one courses to tutored tastings with hundreds of people, Lisa teaches anyone and everyone who wants to delve into the wonderful world of chocolate. Cookery courses have been added recently for people

wanting to expand their sweet and savoury repertoire, and there are opportunities for schools and businesses that can take a tailored approach, from education in the science of chocolate to corporate team building events.

Tutored chocolate tastings or wine and chocolate matching are two of Lisa's favourite events to run for larger groups with her wine merchant husband. You never know where people's taste buds will lead them! She aims to open minds to the world of chocolate and how it has evolved, dismissing the notion that certain types of chocolate are more valid than others and instead embracing the flavour profiles and complexities present in chocolate made with top quality cocoa beans.

"It's really important to me that all my workshops are relaxed, so people don't feel intimidated," says Lisa. "I can talk about the science of tempering chocolate with those who are interested, but at the end of the day we're all there to learn a new skill, have fun, and make and eat chocolates!" Lisa and her assistants are there during every class for hands-on help and encouragement, so whether the students are 10 or 110 years old, they can enjoy an hour or an entire day filled with chocolaty fun.

KNACKALI AND HOW TO TEMPER CHOCOLATE

*Knackali are one of the favourite chocolates taught in our workshops. Here I
share with you how you can make them at home. My students often presume that
tempering chocolate at home will be a disaster — but practise makes perfect! You
certainly don't need any special or expensive equipment!*

125g 33% milk chocolate, finely chopped
75g 70% dark chocolate
*Your choice of toppings such as dried
fruit, nuts, cake decorations or mini
sweets*

Using a plastic bowl (glass holds the heat and spoils the temper) melt the milk
chocolate for 20 seconds in the microwave. Stir the chocolate vigorously then heat
again for 20 seconds. At this stage the chocolate should be completely melted. If it
isn't, put it back in the microwave for 10 seconds at a time, with a vigorous stir in
between each heating, until it is completely melted.

Now add the lump of dark chocolate to the melted milk chocolate. Stir vigorously
for 3 minutes. You are starting a chain reaction of attracting the untempered
crystals in the melted milk chocolate to link up with the tempered crystals still
present in the lump of dark chocolate, all the while cooling the chocolate crystals.

Once the melted and tempered chocolate feels cool to touch, it is ready to use. If
you have a thermometer and the need to be precise, the working temperature of
the melted, tempered chocolate is 30°c.

Use a full teaspoon of chocolate (wiping the bottom of the spoon on the edge of
the bowl to remove the excess) to make 3cm discs of chocolate on baking paper.
We use transfer sheets in the workshop which can be sourced online or purchased
at a workshop. Decorate the discs with your choice of toppings as you go along.

If your chocolate starts to set as you work with it, heat it for 10 to 15 seconds with
the heat of a hair dryer and stir vigorously! Any leftover chocolate can be left to set
as a lump, stored in an airtight container and used next time you make knackali. Or
you could just eat it!

Preparation time: allow half an hour | Makes around 12-15 chocolates

GET ON MY LAND

THE COMMUNITY FARM, LOCATED BETWEEN BRISTOL AND BATH, COMBINES NATURE-FRIENDLY FARMING WITH COMMUNITY ENGAGEMENT TO ENABLE PEOPLE AND GOOD FOOD TO GROW TOGETHER.

The concept of The Community Farm, an idyllic site of 15 acres overlooking Chew Valley Lake, was inspired by a desire to create a resilient local food economy that would benefit people and the environment. From the seeds of this idea, The Farm was founded in 2011: a social enterprise that paired together environmental sustainability and community engagement on a working farm. Unlike most commercial farms in the UK, however, The Community Farm's focus is nature-friendly, and they actively welcome people to 'get on their land' to find out how food is grown.

Alongside growing and selling organic, seasonal, sustainable produce to local communities, there are numerous ways The Farm engages with people. Volunteering is key, with opportunities for regular weekday volunteers, as well as weekend Community Farmer Day events during the growing season. Volunteering helps participants learn first-hand how food, farming, health and wellbeing are interlinked. There are opportunities for people of all ages, abilities and backgrounds to work the land, build new friendships and enjoy some of The Farm's delicious produce, through a shared lunch they pick and prepare together.

During the year, groups of primary school children visit The Community Farm to discover where their food comes from and how it's grown. Picking and tasting produce straight from the fields provides youngsters with knowledge and understanding about how their meals are connected to the land, and to nature. The Farm also hosts a variety of curated events which look to promote positive wellbeing for adults. Amongst these is the therapeutic horticulture course, Grow & Make, a self-referred programme that can be part of a healing process, a learning curve, or just a means to access good food.

Having a positive impact on both people and the environment is central to The Farm's ethos. The organic and nature-friendly methods of farming employed there have fostered a vibrant and biodiverse site. The Farm produces and sources tasty fruit and vegetables for its box delivery customers in Bristol, Bath, Frome, Weston-super-Mare and across the Chew Valley. The scheme also gets fresh produce into Bristol and Bath via The Community Farm's own organic shop, their weigh-and-pay outlet, and a weekly farmer's market. They provide wholesale to retailers and restaurants with similar values, spreading the experience of good farming and good food as wide and far as possible, while always encouraging people to get on their land.

LEEK, POTATO AND CHIVE HASH BROWNS WITH POACHED EGGS

Hash browns are a delicious and hearty breakfast, brunch or side dish. Our version is made with leeks for extra flavour and texture. Make sure you soften them thoroughly before mixing with the potatoes, so they're not crunchy.

1 large leek

1 large baking potato, washed

Salt and pepper

Vegetable or sunflower oil, for frying

Handful of chives, chopped

1 tbsp vinegar

4 eggs

Chilli flakes

Before washing the leek, chop it lengthways into 5cm pieces, then finely slice into thin strips. Place the strips into a big bowl of water and stir with your hand. Leave to stand for a couple of minutes to allow any mud to sink to the bottom of the bowl. While the leek is soaking, grate the potato (without peeling it first) on the large side of the grater into a clean tea towel. Sprinkle the potato with a little salt and leave for 5 minutes before squeezing out as much water as possible.

Scoop the clean leek strips out of the water and roughly dry them. Heat a large frying pan with a splash of oil and gently cook the leek for 5 minutes until soft. Place in a bowl with the grated potato and chopped chives, then add a generous amount of salt and pepper and mix well. Reheat the frying pan with another splash of oil and carefully form the leek and potato mixture into four neat patties. Fry on one side without moving for 5 minutes and then carefully turn over with a spatula and cook for 5 minutes on the other side. Repeat for a further 3 minutes on each side.

While the hash browns are cooking, add the vinegar to a large pan of water and heat. When the water reaches a rolling boil, turn down the heat and carefully crack the eggs into the water. You get a neater poached egg if you first crack them into a small dish or cup so they gently slide into the water. Cook the eggs for 4 minutes (use a timer) and then remove from the water with a slotted spoon. Place immediately on top of the hash browns.

Serve the hash browns and poached eggs alongside toasted bread or a breakfast muffin with a handful of chopped chives, a sprinkle of chilli flakes and black pepper.

This recipe was provided and prepared by award-winning Bristol-based chef, and friend of The Community Farm, Jo Ingleby.

Preparation time: 5 minutes | Cooking time: 25 minutes | Serves: 4

THE
PERFECT
CATCH

FOR THE FRESHEST QUALITY SEAFOOD AT THE RIGHT PRICE IN BRISTOL AND BATH PLUS FILLETING COURSES AND ECO-FRIENDLY LOCAL DELIVERY, THE FISH SHOP IS THE PLACE TO GO.

The Fish Shop specialises in really fresh dayboat fish and seafood from the south coast. There are two locations, Bath and Bristol, which both stock a wide range of shellfish, smoked fish, deli products, sauces and frozen seafood. It was established by Dan Stern in 2010 and has been well supported by local people ever since. The Fish Shop is a chef's back up for a number of prestigious local restaurants such as Bianchi's and Little French.

"We try to buy as local as possible," says Dan. "After nearly a decade in the fish trade we have established contacts in Brixham, Looe, Plymouth and Newlyn fish markets, helping us to source the best in local fish. We are really lucky to be so close to the coast. Our suppliers literally stop and pick up oysters, mussels and crab meat for us on their drive up. We also buy from Fleetwood in Lancashire, Peterhead in Scotland and as far as Shetland."

The 'Var' salmon sold at The Fish Shop comes from the cold waters of the Faroe Islands. It is farmed in a low density free-range manner and guaranteed antibiotic and chemical free. The most local fish on the slab are line-caught from the Chew Valley.

The Fish Shop team are constantly on the lookout for new products too. The most recent example of this is an ancient breed of trout being farmed in Dorset which has twice the Omega 3 of a normal UK farmed trout. The Fish Shop offers selected products for nationwide delivery as well as a more local service in Bristol and Bath via Good Sixty, an eco-friendly bicycle-based food distribution company.

The Fish Shop also offers filleting courses in the evenings. Popular as presents, the two hour course covers all the basics of selecting and filleting fish such as mackerel, sea bass and plaice. Participants also learn to shuck an oyster and clean squid.

From suppliers to customers, Dan is all about good honest service and his favourite thing about working in a shop is the connection he makes with people. "In the Bristol shop we've even seen a first date (where the guy used our fish as the meal's star turn) lead to marriage and now they have a child together. Who knows...but what if he hadn't cooked her a fish supper that day? It's things that like that make this job so worthwhile."

YOUR GUIDE TO BUYING AND

FILLETING FRESH FISH

WHEN BUYING FISH, ALWAYS ASK YOUR FISHMONGER WHAT'S GOOD AND FRESH. IF THEY ARE ANY GOOD, THEY WILL BE DELIGHTED TO TALK YOU THROUGH WHAT'S IN SEASON, WHERE IT'S FROM AND WHEN IT WAS LANDED. YOUR FISHMONGER WILL HAPPILY FILLET YOUR FISH FOR YOU BUT THESE EXTRA TIPS SHOULD ALLOW YOU TO BUY AND THEN FILLET FRESH FISH WITH CONFIDENCE.

BUYING

Fish eyes can be deceptive; the fact that fish is packed and stored in ice means eyes can easily become dull after 24 hours. It's better to look at the gills, as bright red gills are always a good sign. Brown and decaying gills are not. Next, stick your nose in it: fresh fish smells of the sea. Once you've rinsed your hands there should be no discernible fishy taint left. Slimy and stiff is a good thing; if the fish has a slimy bright sheen to it and is still stiff that's a great sign of freshness. Try to avoid fish with guts hanging out, and if the rib cage is lifting away from the fish when it has been gutted that is another bad sign.

When buying shellfish, always ask to see the tags for mussels and oysters so you know how long they have been out of the water. Both can easily last a week or a bit more if looked after properly. You can tell if a mussel is alive by tapping it hard on a board and seeing if it makes any attempt to close.

CLEANING MACKEREL

Lay the fish on its back horizontally in front of you, with the head pointing left for right handers. Run your index finger under the gills and back towards you. Cut in close around the gills, then pinch low and hard to pull out the gills, and discard them.

Now place the fish on the board with the tail furthest away from you. Insert the knife through its anal vent and cut up the length of its belly towards the head. Pull out the guts and discard them. Give the mackerel a quick rinse in cold water and congratulations, you have a gutted fish.

FILLETING MACKEREL

Lay the fish out horizontally again with its gutted belly facing away from you. Lift up the fin just behind its head and cut just behind it at a 45° angle back towards the head, stopping when you reach the back bone. Make a turn and with your knife angled 5% down move along the fish towards the tail with broad strokes until you have released the fillet. Repeat for the other side. Debone both fillets by cutting down just behind the rib cage and scooping or dragging the few larger bones away. You should now have two lovely mackerel fillets. Well done!

For more video tips on fish filleting visit www.lovethefishshop.com/videos

AN EVENT TO REMEMBER

ON THE FOUNDATION OF AN INCREDIBLE HERITAGE, FOSTERS EVENTS HAS REINVENTED ITSELF, BECOMING RELEVANT IN THE FOOD WORLD OF TODAY BUT REMAINING BRISTOLIAN THROUGH AND THROUGH.

Consistently proving that event food doesn't have to be boring and unimaginative, Fosters Events is all about working with clients to develop the perfect menu, whether that's for a marquee wedding in the Cotswolds, a festival-themed corporate party for 1500, creating a street food concept or an intimate ten course tasting menu. Food is at the heart of everything the company does and inspires the team to new creative heights, keeping up to date with Bristol's thriving food scene by eating out around the city, and their menus embody their passion for food.

When Tom Green came on board as chef director in 2016, the move was a catalyst for updating the company's longstanding reputation with fresh influences. Fosters could not operate without the dedicated team that come together to deliver their events. From sales and planning to event delivery and logistics, each individual plays a crucial role in ensuring Fosters events run without a hitch. Fosters works at some of the most iconic venues in the city including Bristol Old Vic, SS Great Britain and Brunel's Old Station and caters for some of the most well-recognised annual events, including Bristol International Balloon Fiesta and Bristol Life Awards.

Celebrating fresh, seasonal, local produce, Fosters uses trusted suppliers but always keeps an ear to the ground for new ones to work with when developing menus and working on bespoke projects. The art of event catering is in creating dishes that can be replicated for thousands of guests at one time; this is a real skill honed by years of combined knowledge.

As clients become more adventurous and look for ways to make their events unique, Fosters is rising to the challenge with the enthusiasm and talent needed to make each one stand out thanks to unforgettable food and excellent service. The praise the team receives for accommodating special dietary requirements should not be overlooked, ensuring each guest feels just as important as the next, and their creativity is visible in every single dish that reaches the table.

Starting life as a wine merchant in 1953, Fosters continues to be an independent, family owned business. It has succeeded in finding a precise balance; proudly retaining its Bristolian heritage and remaining relevant within the food scene today.

LAMB SHOULDER, SMOKED CAULIFLOWER AND SALSA VERDE

Chef's Tip: If the tomatoes have been in the fridge, let them sit on your windowsill for a day or two to get some light, as this will improve the flavour.

1 shoulder of lamb, boned and tied (about 2kg)

Salt and black pepper

250ml chicken stock

10 small bunches of cherry vine tomatoes

2 bunches of asparagus, trimmed (about 500g)

FOR THE CAULIFLOWER PURÉE

2 medium cauliflowers

150g smoked butter

2 medium banana shallots, roughly chopped

500ml double cream

Pinch of ground nutmeg

Pinch of white pepper

FOR THE SALSA VERDE

5 salted anchovy fillets

20g capers

20g baby gherkins (cornichons)

2 cloves of garlic, minced

300ml extra-virgin olive oil

1 tbsp Dijon mustard

1 large bunch of flat parsley, leaves picked

40g mint, leaves picked

40g basil, leaves picked

20ml red wine vinegar

FOR THE LAMB

Set the oven to 100°c. Season the lamb copiously then brown in a large pan over a medium heat. Place the lamb in a deep ovenproof dish with the stock, cover with greaseproof and seal with tin foil. Cook for 10 to 12 hours. When the lamb is cooked it will be soft and easy to cut. Remove the meat from the pan, retaining the liquid, and leave to cool for 15 minutes.

Put on a pair of clean rubber gloves and roll out at least 50cm of cling film on a clean surface. Break the meat down on the cling film and form a large compact 'sausage' with 5cm of space around each edge. Pull the nearest edge of the cling film up and over the meat and tuck it down on itself. Roll the lamb sausage tightly using as much cling film as required (probably about three meters). Tie the ends tightly when you have a compact shape. Cool and refrigerate.

Roast the tomatoes on the vine until they collapse. Blanch the asparagus until al dente, then refresh in iced water. When you are ready to serve, reheat the asparagus in a pan with a little butter.

FOR THE CAULIFLOWER PURÉE

Break the cauliflower into manageable even chunks. Place the butter in a deep saucepan over a medium heat, then add the shallots and cook until translucent. Add the cauliflower and cook until soft but without colour, stirring regularly. Add the cream along with the nutmeg, white pepper and salt to taste. Cook while stirring until the cauliflower is cooked through and the cream has reduced to a thick consistency. Blend to form a purée.

FOR THE SALSA VERDE

Finely chop the anchovies, capers, gherkins and garlic. In a food processor, blend half the olive oil with the mustard and all the herbs (just the picked leaves). Whizz until a paste is formed, then add the chopped ingredients, red wine vinegar and remaining olive oil. Season the salsa to taste, bearing in mind the saltiness of the anchovies.

TO SERVE

Simply use the juices from the lamb tray to make a gravy, thickening if required. Portion the lamb into the desired amounts, place them on a greaseproof lined tray and cook until reheated. The required oven temperature will depend on the portion size, but 180°c is a good starting point. If you have a cooking thermometer, use that to ensure the lamb is over 75°c. Plate the lamb with the roasted tomatoes, asparagus, cauliflower purée, salsa verde and gravy.

Preparation time: 30 minutes | Cooking time: 10-12 hours | Serves: 10 (generously)

THE BEST OF
BOTH
WORLDS

GOOD SIXTY DELIVERS PRODUCE FROM 'HIGH STREET HEROES' IN BRISTOL AND BATH BY ECO-FRIENDLY BIKE, HELPING COMMUNITIES FLOURISH AND ARTISANS CONNECT WITH CUSTOMERS.

The marriage of convenience and shopping with a conscience has been brought about by an initiative launched in Bristol at the end of 2016, which has taken off with such success it has since expanded to Bath and London's Borough Market. Good Sixty is an online platform that enables people to easily purchase groceries from a range of independent food retailers and artisanal producers, which is then delivered to their door. The service has now partnered with over 50 small businesses, delivering fresh produce using their electric cargo bikes in Bristol and collaborating with eco-friendly service, Three Bags Full, to deliver to customers in Bath.

The venture's vision is to create wealthier, better connected communities by helping the smaller fish compete in the large pond of consumerism. By making the average person's whole weekly shop available via online shopping and fuss-free delivery, Good Sixty has a positive impact on the neighbourhoods it operates in, and feeds far more profit back into the local economy. The idea was implemented in Bristol by Good Sixty's founder, Chris Edwards, who saw a need to make ethical and sustainable methods of shopping more accessible. He has lived on Bristol's Gloucester Road since childhood, and was troubled by the number of supermarket delivery vans on his road, despite the number of great independent shops that exist in the area.

However, not everyone has the time to visit all the shops they'd like to and find ethical, eco-friendly and local alternatives to the convenience of that supermarket delivery, so that's where Good Sixty comes in. The website allows you to search by individual business, or shop by category, so you can easily browse and buy at any time. There is a click and collect option, but you can also have your shopping delivered by the collective's eco-friendly cargo bikes, and it won't cost you any more to order from ten different shops than from just one. The cyclists tour the city to make collections at the retailer's preferred times, then bring it all to your home.

The 'High Street Heroes' championed by Good Sixty can be anything from greengrocers to micro-distilleries, fishmongers to bakers. They can even be messaged directly through the website, so you can ask your butcher to prepare steaks in a particular way just as you would in the shop. If you're stuck for inspiration or just want to try something new, there are also bundles of produce – such as a Craft Beer Discovery Box from Bristolian wine merchant Grape and Grind, or Meatbox's Sunday Breakfast Roast Box – to make your weekly shop even easier, and for those looking to send ethical gifts further afield to foodie friends and family around the country, Good Sixty has launched an 'Artisans by Post' service showcasing and posting produce from the very best small-scale producers Britain has to offer.

Nurturing the relationship between producers and customers is a big part of Good Sixty's ethos, and the website reflects that by offering such a bespoke shopping experience. The collective prides itself on a personable approach, so there are digital shop fronts for every one of the High Street Heroes to convey the personality, passion and knowledge of producers as well as explaining more about the journey their products make from beginning to end. These journeys are often very short when it comes to actual food miles, because Good Sixty emphasises local produce as part of its commitment to sustainable shopping that's better for the planet and the economy.

Green initiatives have been in place since the beginning, including the carbon neutral and zero emission delivery system that tackles the twinned problems of air pollution and congestion in cities. There's much more to a truly sustainable business model than that though, as Good Sixty also encourages plastic-free packaging and many customers have already commented on how little waste they find with their deliveries. It also partners with zero-waste shops like Zero Green in Bristol to promote this agenda even further. Seasonality is an important factor in reducing food waste, and this goes hand-in-hand with the local growers and suppliers the website is promoting.

These commitments make a real difference to the cities, customers and businesses that form Good Sixty communities. Every pound spent in this way benefits the local economy 60% more than shopping in a large supermarket. Founder Chris explains: "The service we provide is an essential tool for small food businesses in this digital age, helping retailers and producers share their passion, reach new customers and therefore compete with the 'Big Guys'. Consumer demand for better, ethical, convenient food is at an all-time high and it has been proven time and again: shopping locally has a positive impact on our neighbourhoods, ploughing money back into the local economy and strengthening communities."

With the number of customers and partners growing in Bristol and Bath, his initial vision is fast becoming a reality and the movement is spreading thanks to its popularity, which was demonstrated by the crowdfunding campaign that brought Good Sixty to Bath after reaching 125% of its target, and will extend even further with the introduction of Good Sixty in London for Borough Market's many independent stallholders. Shopping ethically in these cities has never been easier, bringing a whole host of benefits to both sides and allowing them to be better connected for a thriving future.

YOU HAD
ME AT
MERLOT

THE AWARD-WINNING SHOP ON BRISTOL'S BUSTLING GLOUCESTER ROAD OFFERS A HAND-PICKED SELECTION OF WINES, LOCAL CRAFT BEERS, INTERNATIONAL SPIRITS AND COFFEE – HENCE THE NAME – IN A FRIENDLY PLACE TO FIND YOUR FAVOURITE TIPPLE.

Grape & Grind has been well established in Bristol for nine years now, but the seeds were sown years before owner Darren even opened the shop. His career in the wine industry was sparked by a personal interest and progressed via a wine course taken alongside his initial job in engineering, and then a move to Harvey Nichols. He worked in the trade for ten years, learning from an 'inspirational' independent run by an Australian woman, and considering setting up his own business with his wife Polly.

The catalyst came when the couple needed to move house, and when they decided on Bristol it seemed that fate welcomed them in. The closure of several large wine merchant chains on the same street – Gloucester Road – gave Darren's independent shop the perfect opening to provide people with something the supermarkets didn't. Grape & Grind could showcase smaller producers with diverse varieties of wine alongside the European classics. It also branched out to offer great selections of carefully chosen craft beers – championing many Bristol breweries – alongside spirits, including the best-selling Psychopomp Gin, and whiskies from as far afield as Japan and Sweden.

When Darren first got involved with the trade, more traditional wine merchants could be criticised for somewhat stuffy, pretentious attitudes. At Grape & Grind, the exact opposite is encouraged, giving customers an easy and open place to browse and shop with the manager Rob and other members of staff who are happy to chat about the products available. They have a wide range of knowledge to share, and all follow the ethos that buying good drink doesn't have to be an exclusive privilege just for those 'in the know' or with cash to splash.

Having been listed in the 'Top 50 Indies' by Harpers for three years running – a UK wide line up of the best in the business – Grape & Grind is still on an upwards trajectory and a well-loved feature of Bristol's food and drink scene. Plans for the future keep the business on its toes, with the potential introduction of refill bottles for buying wine on tap as part of an ongoing drive to explore more environmentally friendly ways of commerce. The drive behind Grape & Grind's growth has always been Darren's genuine passion for the industry, which keeps his customers engaged and exciting things developing at the shop with each new year.

WINE PAIRINGS

WE'VE PUT TOGETHER SOME THOUGHTS ON THE BEST WINES TO ACCOMPANY SELECTED RECIPES FROM THIS BOOK, SO YOU CAN TURN ANY MEAL OR EVEN PUDDING INTO A SPECIAL OCCASION.

The Lazy Dog – Mackerel, Peach, Quinoa, Cucumber and Dill

Telmo Rodriguez 'Gaba do Xil' Godello, Valdeorras 2017

This is a fabulous dish with plenty of strong flavours and different textures. It requires a white wine that can handle those flavours but in no way overpowers them. Telmo Rodriguez is one of the superstar winemakers of Galicia in north west Spain dedicated to saving and promoting grape varieties such as Godello and Mencia. We think this perfumed Godello with hints of exotic fruit, apple, citrus and white flower should be a perfect match. The ripe, textural and complex palate has a stone fruit minerality, lifted herbal notes and crisp acidity, with white spice and a lengthy finish.

Rosemarino – Seafood Saffron Fregola

Punica Samas, Isola dei Nuraghi Sardinia 2017

So often when we're asked to match a wine with a specific dish, we consider its origins and what wines are produced and have been served with that dish, often for hundreds of years. This fregola has firm roots in Sardinian cuisine, and in this case a Sardinian wine works perfectly. Situated in the south west of Sardinia in an area known as Sulcis Meridionale, this white has lovely refreshing acidity with concentrated pear, apple and apricot flavours. While primarily about crisp fruit characters, there is a touch of minerality and an almost waxy texture here. A blend of 80% Vermentino and 20% Chardonnay, the Vermentino has all the delicate and subtle flavour while the Chardonnay adds that depth and weight needed for this richly aromatic dish.

Root – Beetroot, Hazelnuts and Blackberries

Cret de Garanche Brouilly 2018

Chef Rob Howell describes the beetroot as a humble vegetable, but what a flavour it manages to create: the combination of sweet and earthy is unmistakable. Gamay as a variety is having a huge resurgence, and can be anything from light, fresh and juicy to deep, brooding and altogether much more serious. This Brouilly sits somewhere in the middle of that spectrum and is one of the finest expressions of the grape we've tasted: classic strawberry and raspberry fruit with a touch of savoury on the palate and a very mellow, smooth finish.

WINE PAIRINGS

WE'VE PUT TOGETHER SOME THOUGHTS ON THE BEST WINES TO ACCOMPANY SELECTED RECIPES FROM THIS BOOK, SO YOU CAN TURN ANY MEAL OR EVEN PUDDING INTO A SPECIAL OCCASION.

Pasture – Beef Shin and Ale Pie

Combel la Serre 'Le Pur Fruit du Causse' Cahors 2018

A classic autumn-winter dish that requires a suitably full flavoured but not necessarily blockbuster style of wine. We're long admirers of this Cahors from the south west of France – traditionally Cahors is famous for producing dense black wines from Malbec (yes, Malbec is from France not Argentina originally) – full of tannin and only drinkable after ten years. A new generation is managing to tame Malbec by picking it later and doing less, not trying to extract the last drop of everything from the grapes. Julien Ilbert is squarely in this second group and his wines from pure Malbec are wonderfully fruity and approachable, but with enough rich dark fruit to work perfectly with this hearty pie.

Brace & Browns – Seared Venison Loin with Truffle Mash and Blackberry Red Wine Sauce

Reverdito Nebbiolo, Langhe 2016

One of our favourite dishes, but also one that requires a bit of thought when it comes to a great wine match. We think elegance over bold, powerful reds is the way to go with this lean, flavoursome meat. Nebbiolo is the grape that produces Barolo, Italy's most celebrated red wine. Most producers also make a lighter and more approachable style from younger vines, like this example from Reverdito which is ruby red in colour with intense notes of violet and rose, accompanied by the freshness of ripe red berry fruits on the nose. This is an elegant Nebbiolo complemented by silky tannins and delicate acidity that will balance the red wine sauce in the recipe perfectly.

Joe's Bakery – Portokalopita

Cabidos 'Saint Clement' Petit Manseng Doux, Tolosan 2015

Having a small glass of sweet wine to accompany dessert always feels a little hedonistic, but when you get a perfect match there is nothing quite like it. We're huge fans of this wine from the rolling countryside near the Pyrenees. Made from late picked Petit Manseng grapes, this wine is sweet but light, not at all cloying and is balanced with a tingling freshness and hints of ripe apricot. So good you can definitely stretch to two glasses.

FROM
FIELD
TO FORK

HARTLEY FARM SHOP AND KITCHEN IS A HAVEN FOR FRESHLY GROWN, REARED,
COOKED AND BAKED PRODUCE IN A RURAL IDYLL NOT FAR FROM BATH.

With five generations and over a century of farming experience to their name, the Bowles family who own and run Hartley Farm are passionate advocates for good food. They opened a farm shop on their land in 2008 during a rejuvenation of the working farm, transforming the former arable land into pasture on which they raise grass-fed native breed beef. This is still their main family enterprise, although they now employ over 80 people at the shop thanks to its growth over the years. Hartley Farm is also home to other local producers including a vegetable grower and a sourdough bakery.

Everything produced on the farm is sold in the shop, where a full butcher's counter sources and prepares whole animal carcasses using traditional methods, including Hartley's own meat. Fruit, vegetables, bread, cupboard goodies such as jams and preserves and much more graces the shelves, but everything has one thing in common: provenance is paramount. If you want to taste-test the quality for yourself, all you need to do is head over to Hartley Farm's café where much of the menu can be bought in the shop.

The coffee served in the café is roasted bespoke for Hartley Farm by Origin Coffee of Cornwall, which is blended with organic Jersey milk from Ivy House Farm, a nearby dairy also owned and run by members of the family. The bakery's homemade cakes are the perfect partner, but if you're gearing up for the day a classic farmhouse breakfast can't be beaten. It features Hartley Farm's homemade sausages, locally cured bacon and free-range eggs alongside the sourdough baked onsite. The café is open from morning till afternoon every day, offering seasonal dishes over lunch that stand apart from standard fare thanks to the quality of ingredients and emphasis on freshly prepared food.

In 2015 a second farm shop and kitchen site was added on the beautiful Neston Park Estate just under ten miles away. The focus remains the same: sourcing, producing and serving the very best local food in a beautiful rural setting. Both the venues are 'small but perfectly formed' converted barns, and the seating looks out over the farmland alongside the traditional oak framed buildings. The Bowles family wanted to create a destination with food at the forefront, where people can pop in for their weekly shop as well as relaxing over a delicious meal; the National Farmer's Weekly award for Food Farmer of the Year scooped by Hartley Farm in 2015 is a testament to their success.

Sourdough by ⌂ the oven

made on the farm

CAFE

BEEF FILLET-TAIL STROGANOFF

This is real comfort food. Best of all though, it's dead simple and quick to make and lets
the ingredients do the talking. I use fillet tail here, which is cheaper than fillet steak with
no compromise on tenderness. All good butchers should have it available. This recipe is
based on one of the first dishes I learned to cook but it still remains a go-to favourite.

500-600g grass-fed beef fillet tail
Salt and freshly ground black pepper
A little plain flour for dusting
1 large red onion
350g chestnut mushrooms
50g butter
2 tbsp paprika
300ml crème fraîche
½ a lemon
Handful of parsley, finely chopped

Cut the fillet tails across the grain into thin strips around 3 to 5cm long and season with cracked black pepper. Dust with a little flour, mix everything together and set to one side.

Thinly slice the onion and mushrooms, then add a knob of butter to a non-stick frying pan on a medium heat. Add the onion and cook gently, then stir in the paprika and continue cooking down until the onion is soft and tender. As it begins to soften, add the sliced mushrooms and fry for another 3 to 4 minutes. Then transfer the onions and mushrooms onto a plate.

Turn the heat under the frying pan up to high, add another knob of butter then fry the prepared fillet quickly until browned. Don't overcrowd the pan; fry in batches if needed so the meat doesn't stew. You want a nice brown crust from the flour on the meat, leaving it tender and blushing inside.

Transfer the steak to a plate, add the mushrooms and onions back to the frying pan on a medium heat again, and then add the crème fraîche. Bring the mixture to a gentle simmer until it begins to thicken. Make sure you scrape the bottom of the pan to incorporate all of the beautiful cooking residue from the meat and onions.

Add the beef back to the pan, squeeze in the lemon juice, stir through the chopped parsley and then remove from the heat. Season the stroganoff to taste with salt and pepper. Best served with rice, french fries or even pasta such as pappardelle.

Preparation time: 10 minutes | Cooking time: 20 minutes | Serves: 4-6

SUSTAINING BRISTOL

BROTHERS CHARLIE AND PHIL JAMES HAVE REJUVENATED A COLLABORATIVE SPACE ON JAMAICA STREET IN BRISTOL, CREATING A KITCHEN AND BAR THAT SERVES FOOD AND DRINK INSPIRED BY SUSTAINABILITY AND LOCAL PRODUCE.

Jamaica Street Stores re-opened in September 2019 following a refurb and a rethink about what the place could do for people, and not just customers enjoying its food and drink. Part modern British bistro, part occasion venue, and certainly more than a restaurant, the venture is unique and yet has homely food at its heart. Owners Charlie and Phil James are brothers, and created the menus by reminiscing about what they grew up cooking, eating and drinking in the West Country as well as taking inspiration from the fantastic ingredients produced in and around Bristol.

The biggest emphasis is placed on locality and sustainability at Jamaica Street Stores. "It's absolutely paramount," says Charlie, and just makes sense to us when there's so much in the region to source." Influences find their way into the food from a wide range of cuisines further afield too, putting nduja alongside Fowey mussels and coriander rice with fried Somerset chicken: a firm favourite with diners. The food invites a mix of people as eclectic as the flavours, demonstrating the restaurant's commitment to accessibility so that anyone can walk in and enjoy a drink or a bite to eat.

There's a certain ambiguity in the name and the concept of Jamaica Street Stores, which was a deliberate decision on the owners' part, because they wanted people to see the venue and concept as more than a restaurant. Within the same space exists a DIY supermarket, a plant shop and an exhibition of screen prints for people to explore. The owners of these small businesses work closely with Charlie and Phil and even host occasional events together.

With its minimal industrial design, softened by plenty of greenery and broken up by original features in the Grade II listed former carriageworks, Jamaica Street Stores is an atmospheric place to have a party. Large groups are always welcome to eat and drink, and the whole venue can be hired out too. The venture also has its own music nights, and a range of tipples to make any day a celebration! The extensive wine list focuses on those produced with minimal intervention, alongside lots of canned beer, homemade sodas and spirits which come in pouches, all reducing the bar's environmental impact (as glass bottles take significantly more energy to recycle) in line with the general ethos of sustainability and, of course, with sourcing the most delicious things to eat and drink they can find!

SMOKEY TROTTER BEANS

All our beans and pulses at Jamaica Street Stores come from Hodmedods, who are based in Norfolk. Your butcher will be able to source you trotters with a little notice, don't be scared! We serve this with crispy pork belly at the restaurant. At home it goes on toast smothered in cheese. Make a big batch as they will freeze really well.

400g dried red haricot beans

1 tsp bicarbonate of soda

1 pig trotter

50g unsalted butter

100ml good rapeseed oil

20g ground coriander

15g ground cumin

15g ground fennel

30g smoked paprika

2 red onions, finely diced

3 sticks celery, finely diced

4 cloves of garlic, finely sliced

1 leek, finely diced and washed

2 carrots, peeled and finely diced

800g chopped tomatoes

Salt and pepper, to taste

Soak the dried red haricot beans in two litres of water and the bicarbonate of soda overnight. The next day, drain and rinse the beans.

Place them in a large saucepan with the trotter and cover with fresh water. Bring to the boil and cook for 40 minutes or until the beans are tender. Add more water if necessary but it's important not to add salt at this stage.

While the beans are cooking, melt the butter with the oil in a separate pan, then add the spices and cook gently for 3 to 5 minutes until they are really aromatic.

Add all the diced veg and garlic to the spices and sweat until they turn translucent. The slower you can do this the better. Turn the heat up to medium high and let the vegetables colour slightly, stirring regularly.

Drain the beans, retaining the cooking stock, then add the beans and just enough stock to the vegetables and spices.

If you feel like you're up to it, pick the meat and fat from the cooked trotter, discarding bones and cartilage, then roughly chop it and add into the beans. This is by no means essential, but we think it's worth the time and effort!

Add the tinned tomatoes and simmer gently for a further 20 to 30 minutes so all the flavours mingle. Season the beans to taste with salt and pepper. They are ready to eat right now, but as with any braised dish of this ilk, a day in the fridge will do them nothing but good.

Preparation time: 10 minutes, plus overnight soaking | Cooking time: approx. 1 hour | Serves: 4-6

SOMETHING OLD,
SOMETHING NEW

JOE'S BAKERY COMBINES TRADITION WITH INNOVATION TO CONTINUE
PROVIDING BRISTOLIANS WITH PROPER BREAD, PASTRIES AND SWEET TREATS
FROM THE TWO SHOPS ON GLOUCESTER ROAD.

Martin and Jane Hunt have owned Joe's Bakery for nearly 30 years, during which time they have ensured the long-established business keeps thriving by creating new craft and artisan products as well as preserving the traditions of its long history. There has been a bakery on the same spot since the 1800s, which has been known as Joe's since the 1970s. Since Martin and Jane, along with many others in the area, grew up knowing its good reputation, they kept the name that was recognisable to generations of people who return time and again to the high street bakery.

They have preserved many aspects of a traditional neighbourhood bakery, but combine this with a desire to innovate. "We are always looking for the next thing that people might want, while making sure the quality meets the same high standards we have always worked to," says Martin. Joe's was the first bakery in Bristol to introduce the now incredibly popular sourdough, and has recently begun offering American-style potato rolls which are the next big thing for burger aficionados. The wide range of customers – families, students, tradespeople, workers – are catered for with an ever-expanding selection of craft, artisan and classic breads as well as confectionary.

Inspiration for new products often comes from Martin and Jane's travels – especially when they are exploring cake shops and bakeries around Europe – alongside the favourites that everyone loves such as pies, pasties, Eccles Cakes and other regional classics. Certain ingredients are quite specialist because of this, but most of the flour used at Joe's is sourced much closer to home, from Hosegoods Mill in Avonmouth. Some products are sourced from local suppliers too, but 95% of what they sell is made by the team in-house at the two bakery sites.

The bakery manager, Wayne, also goes on courses to further expand his knowledge and allow him to bring back new ideas. Outside the kitchen, shop manager Jenny is the face of Joe's Bakery alongside owner Jane. The second smaller shop further down Gloucester Road also does takeaway food six days a week, morning until evening, so whether you're after a bread or a brownie Joe's is the place to go! It's a true institution in Bristol, where everyone has their favourite sandwich, cake or loaf and enjoys the marriage of tradition and forward-looking that Joe's embodies.

PORTOKALOPITA

This recipe was gleaned from a very friendly Greek lady as she prepared it for Easter celebrations in a coastal Laconian village. She was proud to pass on her family recipe to us, and we are sure you will be delighted with the result when you try it.

290g sunflower oil

280g sugar

6 medium eggs

1 tbsp vanilla extract

2 tbsp baking powder, mixed with a little water

440g 5% fat Greek yoghurt

500g ready-made filo pastry (fresh or frozen then fully defrosted)

FOR THE SYRUP

2 large oranges, zested and juiced

Equal amount of caster sugar by weight to juice and zest

You will need a 30 by 20cm ovenproof dish or deep baking tray for this recipe. Make and bake it the day before serving, as it needs to stand overnight after baking.

Blend the sunflower oil, sugar, eggs, vanilla extract, baking powder paste and Greek yoghurt together in a large bowl.

Unroll the filo pastry and lift up one sheet using both hands. Dip the filo sheet into the yoghurt mixture to fully coat it, and then fold it into the dish or pan so that it forms 'waves' about 3 to 4cm high. Ruck the pastry up as you go and slide it to one end of the pan.

Continue dipping and folding until all the filo is used up. Rearrange the pastry so that it is evenly spaced in the dish. Discard the remaining yoghurt mixture, then leave the portokalopita to rest for 30 minutes. Preheat the oven to 180°c when the resting time is nearly up.

FOR THE SYRUP

Stir the equal amounts of sugar and orange zest and juice together in a small saucepan. Gently boil the syrup, stirring occasionally, until it has reduced to a medium-thick consistency, then take off the heat.

Bake the rested portokalopita in the centre of the preheated oven for 30 minutes. The 'custard' should now have set but still be a little wobbly. If it is still runny, bake for a few more minutes then check again. Spoon (or slowly pour) the syrup evenly over the portokalopita while it is still hot, allowing it soak in as you go. Leave the dessert to cool, then cover with a clean cloth and leave to stand overnight.

Cut the portokalopita to size with a sharp knife. You should be able to press out a little of the orange syrup from the cut squares. This is a good test that you have the right amount.

Serve on its own or with Greek yoghurt. Enjoy!

Preparation time: 15 minutes, plus 30 minutes resting | Cooking time: 30 minutes | Serves: 12-15

A MAN'S
BEST
FRIEND

THE LAZY DOG IS A TRUE LOCAL THAT OFFERS A FRIENDLY WELCOME FOR PEOPLE OF ALL AGES, ALONGSIDE CAREFULLY CURATED MENUS OF FOOD AND DRINK THAT STRADDLE THE LINE BETWEEN MODERNITY AND TRADITION.

In a time when good old-fashioned pubs are fewer and further between, The Lazy Dog is a beer-led yet family-friendly haven that also does proper food, from ham, egg and chips to a cracking Sunday roast. Definitively local (as opposed to 'destination' watering holes) and not a gastropub, it has been around for almost a decade and was the third instalment of a trilogy from owners Mike Cranney and Joby Andrews, following The Pipe & Slippers and The Windmill. Matt Bolton has run The Lazy Dog since 2012 with a shared ethos of 'reinventing a classic boozer' which means retaining everything that makes a traditional pub great, while embracing certain things in addition.

These include a friendly welcome for visitors young and old; The Lazy Dog is just off Gloucester Road and surrounded by residents of all ages, so it's important to Matt and the team that the pub provides something for everyone. The upstairs room can be hired out for activities and also plays host to film nights and comedy clubs. The large walled garden is a lovely place to sit and sip in the sun, and when the weather's at its most British a sheltered area still makes the most of the outdoor space. Local football and cricket teams are sponsored by the pub too, highlighting the genuine aim for The Lazy Dog to stay community-focused.

This approach is mirrored in the pub's food and drink, which is all carefully selected to make sure it's top quality as well as supporting local businesses, such as suppliers and producers, as much as possible. There are wines chosen by real wine lovers without the exorbitant prices, non-alcoholic drinks that are not just for children, and crowded shelves inspired by gin palaces of old. The bar is very much beer-led, with regular draft options from the likes of Bristol Beer Factory and Lost and Grounded plus a range of national and international products.

The food menus also strike a happy balance between culinary influences near and far, featuring pub classics such as fish and chips, steaks and burgers with a smattering of head chef Nick Delgado's Chilean heritage. As a modern establishment and a community pub, The Lazy Dog has just about everything you want with a 'quality not quantity' approach. You can drop by for a pint or bring the whole family for a three course meal; either will be equally welcomed and provided for in this proud independent.

MACKEREL, FLAT PEACH, QUINOA, CUCUMBER AND DILL SALSA

Quick to prepare, this dish is a wholesome plate of food that's packed with goodness without compromising on flavour.

160g quinoa

1 cucumber

1 red chilli

¼ bunch of flat leaf parsley

¼ bunch of coriander

½ bunch of dill

50ml extra-virgin olive oil

2 limes, juiced

Pinch of salt

2 flat peaches, pitted and halved

4 fillets of mackerel

Knob of butter

Rinse the quinoa under cold running water for a few minutes, then lightly toast it in a saucepan until it starts to brown. Submerge the toasted quinoa in about twice as much salted water. Bring to the boil and then simmer for about 10 to 15 minutes until the water has been absorbed and the kernels have popped open.

While the quinoa is cooking, finely dice the cucumber and chilli, chop the parsley, coriander and dill and gently mix them all together. Add the olive oil and the lime juice, mix and then season to taste.

Preheat the oven to 180°c. Put a griddle pan on a medium heat, add the peach halves and cook for 2 or 3 minutes on each side then set aside. Add some oil to the pan and place the mackerel fillets in, skin side down. Put the pan into the oven, cook the mackerel for 2 to 3 minutes, then take it out and add the butter to the pan. Set aside to rest briefly before you plate the food.

TO SERVE

Place a pile of quinoa in the centre of the plate, put two mackerel fillets on top, add two peach halves on the side and drizzle salsa on top of the fish and around the plate.

A STORY OF
FOOD AND FARMING

LUKE HASELL'S JOURNEY THROUGH FOOD AND FARMING HAS AN IMPORTANT MESSAGE AT ITS HEART: TO REMEMBER AND CELEBRATE WHERE OUR FOOD REALLY COMES FROM.

With two butchers, an online meat box business, restaurants, festivals and an organic farm to look after, Luke Hasell is a busy man but also someone for whom good food is a central part of life. He describes his many ventures as "a continuous drive to educate consumers about where our food comes from" but began his journey quite unexpectedly, on inheriting his parents' farm. One of the first changes Luke made was to transform the farming practices so it became completely organic.

He began by rearing beef and later pork as well, realising along the way that he didn't want the hard work that went into producing this superior quality meat to be paid for unfairly by supermarkets. This led to Luke's establishment of The Story, an online meat box business, which soon branched out into butcher's shops in the village nearest the farm and in Bristol. All the meat sold through these outlets is 100% pasture fed – Meatbox is the only Bristolian butcher to do this – so the flavour really shines through.

Having invested in eco-friendly and high quality farming practices, Luke decided to open those ideas up to more people by co-founding The Community Farm. Luke's farm now welcomes thousands of visitors and volunteers each year, offering educational opportunities to get your hands dirty.

Bringing his ethos to the city, Luke then produced the Eat Drink Bristol Fashion festival alongside Michelin-starred chef Josh Eggelton. The flagship event showcased a mix of great restaurants from fine dining to tapas, as well as local producers and live music. Luke and Josh aimed to create unique dining experiences in unusual places, and this led to their launch of Yurt Lush near Temple Meads. The second award-winning Bib Gourmand restaurant, Root, followed in transformed steel containers at Cargo, where head chef Rob Howell helps to shape how people see food, putting the focus on vegetables to redefine ideas of delicious and filling dishes.

Four years on, Luke wanted to bring his love of food back home and so created Valley Fest, 'the best tasting music festival in the south west', which is held next to The Community Farm and alongside Chew Valley Lake. With a chef's table, seasonal banquets and lots of independent traders, it's a feast of locally grown and produced food. All this is thanks to Luke's drive to explore where what we eat really comes from and how we can do it better, along with a host of passionate people who love to eat, cook, grow and celebrate good food.

EAT.
PROPER.
MEAT.

BEEF SHORT RIBS
100% GRASS FED
£ 11.99/kg

BEETROOT, HAZELNUTS AND BLACKBERRIES

This is Root's most iconic dish, which has remained on the menu since we opened.
Chef Rob Howell celebrates the humble vegetable, creating an interesting, simple
and delicious dish.

18 beetroots
20g sea salt
1 punnet of blackberries
100g hazelnuts, roasted
120ml quality white vinegar
60ml water
80g sugar
Drizzle of rapeseed oil
Few nasturtium leaves, to garnish

To make the fermented beetroot, peel and grate seven of the beetroots. Place the grated beetroot in a bowl and add the sea salt. Massage the salt into the beetroot, squeezing to release juice from the vegetable. Make sure there is enough juice released to cover the grated beetroot.

Place the mixture into a container (a four litre ice cream tub would be perfect) and cover with baking parchment. Sit another tub on top of the parchment, weighted down to press the beetroot, making sure the grated veg is submerged in the liquid. Leave in a cool, dry place for 6 days to finish the fermentation process.

Preheat the oven to 200°c. Place ten whole beetroots on a tray and roast them in the oven for 2 hours 30 minutes. Allow them to cool, then you should be able to peel off the skins easily using your hands. Roughly chop the roasted beetroot and place in a bowl. Cut the blackberries and roasted hazelnuts into quarters and place into separate bowls for the moment.

For the pickling liquor, put the vinegar, water and sugar in a saucepan, bring to the boil and whisk before removing from the heat and cooling. Peel and slice the last beetroot thinly on a mandoline and place the discs in the liquid to pickle.

TO SERVE

Place the roasted beetroot and three large tablespoons of fermented beetroot in a mixing bowl. On each dish, plate a large spoonful of the beetroot mix, then scatter the hazelnuts, blackberries and pickled beetroot on top. Dress with some rapeseed oil, a drizzle of the beetroot pickling liquor and a few nasturtium leaves if you can get them.

Preparation time: 1 week | Cooking time: 2 hours 30 minutes | Serves: 6

FRESH IS BEST

NO TRIP TO CLIFTON VILLAGE IS COMPLETE WITHOUT A VISIT TO THE MALL DELI. IT'S A LOCAL INSTITUTION, HAVING OPERATED AS A DELI IN THE HEART OF THE VILLAGE FOR OVER 30 YEARS, AND BEEN RUN AS A DELI AND CAFÉ BY CURRENT OWNER, KATE, FOR THE LAST TEN.

The traditional feel and approach to service remains at The Mall Deli, but what makes it a firm favourite with food lovers is the delicious homemade goodies created daily and the fact that Kate and deli manager, Josie, are passionate about working with local suppliers and showcasing emerging British foods.

The cheese counter is a cheese lover's heaven with a wide variety of British cheeses sourced by Rosie at The Bristol Cheesemonger, while British salamis from Cornish Charcuterie sit alongside traditional gammon ham and rare roast beef joints. Other locally sourced delights include a wide variety of handmade Scotch eggs from Hereford, bakes from The Parsnipship in Bridgend, and raw chocolate tarts from Somerset's Liberty Loves, but the list goes on and on.

Kitchen manager Tim and his team create a huge amount of food daily too, from sausage rolls, quiches, frittatas, salads and sandwiches to cakes and tray bakes, with plenty of veggie, vegan and gluten-free options. Their passion for locally sourced seasonal ingredients is easily satisfied, with fruit and veg arriving daily from another legendary Clifton Village business, Reg The Veg.

The shelves are stocked from floor to ceiling with a vast array of artisan products from independent suppliers based in Bristol, the West Country and Wales. These include Go Wild Preserves, who make their fabulous seasonal jams and chutneys just a few miles away. Gift hampers filled with gorgeous produce are made up ready to go, and customers often put their own bespoke hampers together too. To make it even easier for customers, hampers and lots of other deli bits can be ordered via Good Sixty for local delivery.

While away an afternoon with lunch, coffee and a slice of cake in the café, or choose something to take away from the vast array on offer in the deli – the lunch boxes are very popular. On a busy day the kitchen will bake off several batches, but once it's gone, it's gone - the aim is to sell out and do it all again the next day! The team's welcoming service and food knowledge is renowned, and with its varied and ever-evolving food offering, it's easy to see The Mall Deli going for at least another 30 years.

GOATS' CHEESE & VEGETABLE FRITTATA

A fond favourite at the deli – tasty, light but filling, gluten-free – what's not to love? We vary the flavours daily, but there are some combinations that just fly out. This one is packed full of seasonal veg and kept fluffy by the addition of ricotta. You can substitute the vegetables indicated in the recipe below for any you fancy, just make sure any root veg is pre-roasted and be careful not to use too many high moisture vegetables like courgettes together. You can also replace the goat's cheese with another cheese if you prefer.

2 courgettes, chopped into chunks

2 sweet potato, diced and roasted (peel first if you prefer)

200g peas (frozen is fine)

½ a head of broccoli, thinly sliced

1 red onion, thinly sliced

200g ricotta

12 large free-range eggs

6cm of goat's cheese log (approx 330g) cut into 6 slices

Freshly chopped herbs (such as parsley and chives)

Freshly ground black pepper

Sea salt, to taste

Lightly oil a 23cm cake tin and line it with greaseproof paper.

In a mixing bowl, whisk the eggs with a little seasoning, mix through the ricotta and then add the vegetables and herbs. Stir gently so that the vegetables do not break up.

Pour the mixture into the cake tin, ensuring that the frittata is level and the vegetables are evenly distributed. Lay the slices of goat's cheese on top of the frittata mix.

Bake at 160°c for 30 to 40 minutes. The frittata should brown slightly and feel firm to the touch when done. Allow it to cool for 5 to 10 minutes before removing from the tin and slicing to serve.

Preparation time: approx. 15 minutes | Cooking time: 30-40 minutes, plus roasting time | Serves: 6-8

INDULGENT CHOCOLATE CAKE
WITH SUMMER BERRIES

*This delicious moist cake keeps well, ideal if you want to bake ahead. An added bonus is
that it's vegan, although it is universally enjoyed by all our chocolate-loving customers!
If needed, gluten-free flour and baking powder substitutes can be used too.*

FOR THE BERRY JAM

*250g berries (can be raspberries,
blackberries, strawberries or a mix)*

100g caster sugar

2 tbsp water

FOR THE SPONGE

750ml soya milk (or other non-dairy milk)

250ml olive oil

2 tsp vanilla extract

600g self-raising flour (sifted)

100g cocoa powder

2 tsp baking powder

2 tsp bicarbonate of soda

600g caster sugar

FOR THE CHOCOLATE ICING

250g vegan margarine

75g cocoa powder

100g icing sugar, sifted

2-3 tbsp soya milk

FOR THE DECORATION

*According to personal preference – we
often use fresh berries and chocolate
crumbs or shards*

Preheat the oven to 155°c. Lightly oil two 23cm cake tins, then line them with greaseproof paper. If you are using 20cm sandwich tins, halve the recipe quantities and reduce the baking time by 10 to 15 minutes.

FOR THE BERRY JAM

This can be made ahead of time, but if you are short on time, you can use a jar of jam instead. In a small saucepan, warm the berries, sugar and water over a low heat for approximately 10 minutes, stirring regularly until a jam like consistency is achieved. Set aside to cool until needed.

FOR THE SPONGE

Pour the soya milk, oil and vanilla extract into another saucepan, stir over a gentle heat for a couple of minutes until the mixture is warm and well combined. Sift the flour, cocoa powder, baking powder and bicarbonate of soda into a large bowl and mix to combine. Add the sugar and stir through. Now slowly add the wet ingredients into the dry ingredients, whisking well to ensure that there are no lumps or pockets of flour.

Pour or scrape the batter into the prepared cake tins and bake for 35 to 40 minutes. The cakes are ready when an inserted knife or skewer comes out clean. Allow them to cool completely in the tins before decorating.

FOR THE CHOCOLATE ICING

Use a stand or hand mixer to combine the vegan margarine, cocoa powder and icing sugar until the icing is completely smooth. Add soya milk a tablespoon at a time to achieve your preferred consistency.

TO ASSEMBLE

Take the cooled sponges out of their tins. If they are domed in shape you can slice the peaks off to level them for decoration. Place one sponge on your serving plate and spread a thick layer of icing over it. Add a dollop of berry jam, spreading it out from the centre but leaving 2cm clear around the edge to allow it to spread when you place the second sponge on top. Use the remaining icing to finish the cake as you prefer, either adding another layer of icing on top or icing the top and sides of the cake. We often briefly chill the cake at this point to allow the icing to set slightly before adding decorations like fresh berries, chocolate discs or shards, chocolate crumb, freeze-dried raspberries…we do it slightly differently every time!

Preparation time: 30 minutes | Cooking time: 35-40 minutes | Serves: 10+

YOUR DAILY BREAD

FROM ONE BREAD-MAKING COURSE TO A THRIVING INDEPENDENT BAKERY WITH A CAFÉ AND SHOP ON BRISTOL'S BUSTLING NORTH STREET, THE SUCCESS OF MARK'S BREAD IS AS DOWN TO EARTH AS ITS NAME...

Mark Newman has always been interested in food, so when a 50th birthday present from his wife Maria gave him the opportunity to enjoy three days of bread making, he was inspired to leave a career in IT for the adventure of establishing a bakery. November 2019 saw the tenth anniversary of that venture – aptly named Mark's Bread – after it grew organically thanks to experimentation, visits to other UK bakeries, and a commitment to artisan methods. Following the course that initially sparked his interest, Mark set up the business on his own as a self-taught baker, in a former garage which is now shared with a brewery.

Today, Mark and Maria co-direct the bakery, café and shop on North Street. The business was able to expand into the upstairs and next door spaces to create a community-friendly place that creates, bakes and sells delicious food six days a week. Sourcing the best ingredients is important to the team, who make a variety of sourdough, traditional yeasted and continental breads alongside a daily special, using slow-proving methods and only organic flour. Delicious cakes and a range of sweet and savoury pastries also feature. The bakery has teams of bakers and chefs, a cake and pastry team and a front of house team to cover all aspects of the friendly and welcoming bakery and eatery.

"Our objective is for the people who work with us to enjoy the work, feel able to be creative and take pride in what they do," says Mark. "This is why we're part of the Living Wage Foundation and focus on the quality of everything we make." As much food as possible is made in-house for the renowned breakfast dishes, daily specials, and lunch options including fresh salads, soups and sandwiches. The grocery shelf stocks a seasonal range of homemade jams, chutneys, cereals and more. The range of breads are also sold wholesale to restaurants and cafés within a certain radius, determined by how far the delivery cyclist can go on the custom-made electric bike!

Mark's customers include a Michelin-starred restaurant and the set of BBC's Cornish TV drama, Poldark. Anyone after a delicious celebratory treat can order their unique cake by choosing size, decoration, dietary requirements and collecting the beautiful cake a few days later. The bakery makes gluten-free bread and cake, and the café features plenty of vegan and vegetarian offerings, so there's something for everyone, even bread-making courses run by Mark for those keen to learn or inspired to follow in his footsteps!

PORK PIE

*Here's a bit of food nostalgia; a long time ago while picking hops in Kent I bought
a pork pie from the village shop, sat in an orchard and ate the best pork pie ever.
Since then I've been trying to make a pork pie as good as that one.*

FOR THE FILLING

250g pork belly, minced

250g pork shoulder, diced

45g onion

4g dried sage

2g dried thyme

5g fresh parsley

2g ground nutmeg

4g Dijon mustard

4g black pepper

5g salt

FOR THE HOT WATER PASTRY

120g lard

65g butter

160ml water

420g flour

9g salt

3 egg yolks

FOR THE JELLY

½ sheet of gelatine

200ml chicken or ham stock

FOR THE FILLING

Use good quality free-range pork if you can. We use locally reared pork from the Belmont Estate near Bristol. Finely chop or grate the onion then sweat in a pan for 5 minutes before mixing all the ingredients together in a bowl. The minced belly provides a good fat content which will render down and the diced shoulder provides texture and leaner meat.

FOR THE HOT WATER PASTRY

Heat the lard and butter in the water until melted. Sift the flour and salt into a bowl, stir in the hot liquid then add two of the egg yolks. Knead gently to make a smooth, uniform dough.

TO MAKE THE PIES

Grease a tin or six ramekins and place a disc of greaseproof paper on the base to prevent the pastry sticking. Take a ball of the warm pastry and, using your thumb, line the tin evenly right up to the rim. The pastry should be approximately 3mm thick or thicker for large pies, and 90g of pastry should line a 7cm ramekin to make a pie for one, 130g of pastry should line a 10cm tin.

Fill the pies up to the rim but allow room for the jelly. Roll out a 3mm thick disc of the pastry to make a lid, lay it over the filling and press the edges down with a fork to seal the join. Cut a small hole in the centre of the lid for the jelly.

Brush the pie with the remaining egg yolk and place in a preheated oven at 210°c for 20 minutes, then reduce the temperature to 180°c for an extra hour (or up to 1 hour 30 minutes for larger pies) until the pastry is golden brown.

FOR THE JELLY

Meanwhile, make the jelly by placing the gelatine in the stock and heating gently while stirring to dissolve it.

When the pies have cooled for 15 minutes after cooking, carefully remove them from the tins or ramekins and place on a rack. Fill them with as much jelly as they will take through the hole in the top of the pie. A plastic squeezy bottle with a nozzle is ideal for this, or you can use a small funnel or jug. The jelly stock keeps the filling moist and keeps pork pie purists happy!

Once the pies are cool, refrigerate to set the jelly. Great served with piccalilli.

Preparation time: I hour | Cooking time: I hour 30 minutes | Makes 6 individual pies or I large pie

CHELSEA BUN

Bath has the Bath bun, London the Chelsea bun, and Bristol has the Colston bun, a spiced fruit bun named after Edward Colston who made his wealth from the slave trade. Given the dubious heritage of the Colston bun, here is our recipe for the Chelsea bun.

FOR THE FLYER (OR STARTER)

80g wholemeal bread flour

230ml warm water

8g fresh yeast (or 4g dried yeast)

FOR THE DOUGH

320g white bread flour

5g salt

60g sugar

60g butter, diced

FOR THE FILLING

130g raisins

40g sugar

5g cinnamon

2g allspice

20g butter, melted

FOR THE ICING

200g icing sugar

½ a lemon, zested and juiced

FOR THE FLYER (OR STARTER)

Mix the wholemeal flour with the warm water and yeast to make a light batter. Store the flyer in a warm environment for 30 minutes to 1 hour until it froths.

FOR THE DOUGH

When the flyer is ready, add the white bread flour to it and then knead the dough by hand for 10 minutes (or a few minutes if using a machine) until the gluten starts to develop and the dough begins to stretch.

Add the salt, sugar and diced butter then knead again until all the butter has been incorporated. The dough should have a silky sheen and stretch thanks to the developed gluten. Let the dough rest at room temperature in a covered bowl for a couple of hours, by which time the dough should have doubled in size and wobble like a jelly.

FOR THE FILLING

Soak the raisins in a little water to make them juicy. Combine the sugar, cinnamon and allspice. Flour a work surface and roll the dough into a rectangle approximately 40cm long by 20cm wide. Brush the dough with most of the melted butter, reserving some for coating the final roll. Sprinkle the spice and sugar mix and raisins evenly onto the dough.

Roll the dough up like a swiss roll from the long side, trying to keep the filling evenly distributed and the ends tidy. The roll should be about 40cm long. Brush it with the remaining melted butter and then divide into eight even slices with a sharp knife.

Line a 20cm by 30cm baking tin with greaseproof paper and place the buns evenly into the baking tin cut side up. Prove the buns for another hour and a half until they have expanded and 'kiss' the sides of the others. Bake in a preheated oven at 210°c for about 15 minutes, or until brown.

FOR THE ICING

Mix the icing sugar with the lemon zest and juice, then add water a tiny splash at a time to make a thick but spreadable paste. Coat the buns with the icing while they are still warm using a brush or spatula.

Allow to cool and serve with a cup of tea!

Baker's note: most of the doughs we make are slow fermenting, proved over 24 hours to enhance the flavour, but because the Chelsea bun gets its flavours from added ingredients, a 'quick' dough will suffice. Making a flyer allows the yeast to get going before it battles against other ingredients of the enriched dough, which will slow down fermentation.

Preparation time: 3 hours | Cooking time: 15 minutes | Makes 8 large or 12 small buns

THE BARE
NUTCESSITY
OF LIFE

UNIQUE NUT BUTTERS ARE THE LIFEBLOOD OF A SMALL START-UP WITH BIG IDEAS ABOUT HOW TO MAKE DELICIOUS PEANUT-FREE SPREADS THAT ARE GOOD FOR YOUR BODY, YOUR TASTE BUDS AND THE PLANET.

Nutcessity was established by Mike Duckworth in August 2016. Back then, he'd been thinking about making and selling nut butters for a long time, having first tasted it 'on exchange' at university in Australia, aged 20. This was something of a revelation, seeing as the range of non-peanut spreads available in the UK was limited. A couple of years later, Mike fine-tuned his ideas for creating a business out of this new interest, steered in helpful directions by jobs at Abel & Cole and The Better Food Company in Bristol, after graduating with a degree in International Business.

"Those experiences led me to figure out what kind of product I wanted to make," says Mike, and the result was something entirely unique, even within the increasingly popular nut butter world. Nutcessity currently offers a range of six jarred spreads made from a blend of nuts, seeds, coconut flesh and whole fruit. There's no refined sugar, and all ingredients are certified organic. This lends a different texture to the nut butters, which Mike describes as "a bit creamier and more biscuit-y, less cloying, with a slight sweetness from the natural sugars in the fruit."

The enterprising founder is chef, labeller, delivery man and more for the growing venture. Mike lives and works between Warwick, (where a room in his parents' house has been converted into a purpose-built kitchen to handle all production), and Bristol; where for two days he delivers orders directly to customers and adds to his list of over 40 stockists, which include Better Food, Source Food Hall and Elemental Collective, where the photos opposite were taken. He also spends weekends at markets and food festivals, enjoying the interaction with people who can try and buy his nut butter first-hand. "People in Bristol are great; willing to try new things, happy to give honest feedback and big supporters of independents."

In May 2019, Mike began partnering with FRANK Water (www.frankwater.com), the Bristol-based charity which helps to provide safe drinking water in Nepal and India. Through this, Nutcessity contributes a proportion of profits to the charity each year, while a 'nut butter recipe book' he's created has a fundraising target of £2,500. He hopes to keep expanding all aspects of his small business and bringing the benefits of his organic, peanut-free, delicious and nutritious nut butters to more people in Bristol and beyond.

You can buy Mike's nut butter online at: nutcessity.co.uk.

APPLE & GINGER COOKIEJACKS

*My parents' garden has a huge apple tree, so we always need creative ways to
use our apples in September and October. These cookies (or flapjacks?) are fun
and easy to make, taste fab, and are totally dairy-free.*

4-5 apples

40g ginger (in syrup)

2 Weetabix

*100g Nutcessity gingerbread almond
butter*

50g chopped nuts (I used pecans)

50g jumbo oats

50g porridge oats

50g soft light brown sugar

1 tbsp syrup (from the ginger)

¼ tsp salt

Preheat the oven to 180°c.

Remove the skin from the apples with a knife and set the peel to one side. Core
and then grate the apples so that you have around 200g to use. Add this to a large
mixing bowl.

Finely grate the ginger and add it to the bowl. Finely crumble the Weetabix into the
bowl along with all the other ingredients. Mix well with a wooden spoon or spatula
to bring everything together.

Put a sheet of parchment paper over a baking tray, then with wet hands scoop
the mixture out onto the parchment to form ten even balls of cookie dough. Add
the apple peel to the tray so it doesn't go to waste; when heated and left to dry it
makes a great snack.

Bake the cookiejacks for 15 minutes. The skin is best left to cool, but eat the jacks
warm or cold… Serve with your feet up and a cuppa. What else!

Preparation time: 10 minutes | Baking time: 15 minutes | Makes: 10 cookies

ON TO
PASTURES
NEW

BRISTOL'S RENOWNED STEAKHOUSE AND BAR IS A CELEBRATION OF THE INCREDIBLE EFFECTS CHARCOAL AND FIRE CAN HAVE ON TOP QUALITY MEAT. A BIT OF THEATRE AND A VIBRANT BAR THROWN IN FOR GOOD MEASURE MAKES THIS RESTAURANT A MUST VISIT FOR DISCERNING DINERS.

Pasture is the culmination of chef owner Sam Elliott's twin passions – meat and butchery – and treats ingredients, cooking and customers alike with dedication and respect. Opened in March 2018, the steakhouse and bar is about beautiful, modern food for everyone, which has already been highly praised by food writer Grace Dent and embraced by Bristolians who keep coming back for more.

Having committed to opening his first restaurant in his home town, Sam wanted to use his experience to create something very special in Bristol. Pasture's concept was partly inspired by the building it's housed in, which he fell in love with as soon he walked into the magnificent large Victorian venue. The two spacious levels lend themselves to the theatre of the open kitchen upstairs and the convivial bar area as you walk in on the ground floor.

The menus are as grand yet accommodating as the space. There are lunch options for people not wanting to linger as well as à la carte dishes that range from simple – like crispy squid with garlicky aioli – to sumptuous, such as house cuts of chateaubriand. Influences range from Asian to Argentinian, and Sam explains that there are 'no restrictions' on where their creativity and imagination takes them.

Underpinning this wide-ranging outlook is an ethos based on sustainability, seasonality and quality. It's important to Sam that all the animals he sources are reared ethically, so beef is reared on the moors in Cornwall and then dry-aged for up to 65 days with Himalayan salt blocks in the restaurant. The in-house butchers prepare whole cuts of beef, and the chefs then cook them using a Japanese 'robata' grill over open flames for distinctive flavours and textures.

Head chef, Rhys Grayson, and general manager, Federica Civale, have been with Pasture from its conception and seen the team expand from 17 to 40 people in just over 18 months. Sam aims to continue innovating and working with new suppliers to keep Pasture as fresh as its quarterly changing menus. The extensive cocktail offering, local beers on tap and house gin made in collaboration with Psychopomp Distillery already heighten Pasture's appeal, and the downstairs space is also regularly transformed into a music venue for live sessions and DJs.

The steakhouse and bar has grown from a genius idea to a wonderful reality in an impressively short yet successful period. Pasture adheres to Sam's endless dedication to quality and sustainability which hasn't come at the expense of entertainment – and, of course, fantastic food, drink and ambience – for everyone who visits.

THE ULTIMATE STEAK!

Our signature dish at Pasture is the tomahawk steak. The tomahawk is a cut from the rib and is essentially a large ribeye steak served on the bone. It's shaped like a tomahawk axe, hence the name. Here we will tell you everything about selecting the best steaks, cooking and serving them.

SELECTING YOUR STEAK

In our opinion the best beef comes from cattle raised naturally on pasture (a diet of grass and hay) and should have been aged for at least 21 days for the tenderness. Dry aged would always be our preference for the best flavour!

COOKING YOUR STEAK

Now you have selected your steak, the best way to cook it would be over hot coals. A kettle barbecue is best for this as it has a lid. Take your steaks out of the fridge 30 minutes prior to cooking. Light the barbecue and position the coals to one side of the grill. Once the coals are hot and have a good covering of white embers you are ready to cook.

Season the steak all over with salt and pepper and rub with olive oil. Place the steak over the hot coals and sear the steak on both sides. This should take about 5 to 10 minutes. (If the grill flares up position the steaks away from the direct heat until the flames settle down.) Once nicely browned, move the steak away from fierce coals so it cooks by indirect heat, place the lid on the barbecue and leave for 10 minutes, turning half way through.

Once the desired internal temperature has been achieved (see below), remove the steak from the grill and leave to rest for 10 minutes. This allows the juices to soak back into the meat and keep it tender.

TEMPERATURE GUIDE

Medium-rare: 40-45°c
Medium: 45-50°c
Medium-well done: 50-55°c

These guidelines are about 5°c lower than the norm, which is due to the resting time and residual heat in the bone of the tomahawk steak. The temperature will naturally increase during resting.

FOR THE CHIMICHURRI SAUCE

1 tsp salt
50ml boiling water
1 bunch of curly parsley
1 small bunch of oregano
4 cloves of garlic
100ml water
100ml pomace oil
50ml red wine vinegar
1 tsp dried chilli flakes

FOR THE CHIMICHURRI SAUCE

Dissolve the salt in the boiling water, then allow to cool before starting to blend. Add all the ingredients to a blender and blitz until smooth. The sauce should be slightly sour to help cut through the fattiness of the steak. Add chilli flakes to taste. Slice the steak and serve with lashings of chimichurri sauce.

Preparation time: 20 minutes | Cooking time: 45 minutes | Serves: 6

BEEF SHIN AND ALE PIE

Step up your pie game with our twist on the classic steak and ale pie. This serious pie is great for dinner parties and will be sure to get your guests' full attention. It's deeply flavoured and rich with buttery flaky pastry, paired with fresh herbs and pickles to elevate the whole dish.

FOR THE ROUGH PUFF PASTRY

250g butter, frozen

250g plain flour

5g salt

2 eggs, beaten

FOR THE FILLING

125g chestnut mushrooms

20 silverskin onions

2 tbsp beef dripping

4 cloves of garlic

2 carrots, roughly chopped

2 sticks of celery, sliced

1 onion, diced

1 tbsp tomato purée

2 sprigs each of rosemary and thyme

2 bay leaves

750g diced beef shin

2 tbsp plain flour

Salt and pepper

1 can of Guinness or good stout

500ml beef stock

4 x 5cm marrow bones, cleaned

FOR THE GARNISH

2 sprigs each of tarragon and chervil

2 shallots, finely sliced

4 chestnuts, peeled

25ml red wine vinegar

FOR THE ROUGH PUFF PASTRY

Freeze the butter until hard then grate into a bowl. Combine the grated butter with the flour and salt, then make a small well in the mixture and slowly add 100ml of water while stirring with a round-bladed knife until the pastry comes together. You will need to work fast as you don't want the butter to melt while making the pastry. Wrap the pastry in parchment paper and chill.

Once chilled, lightly flour the pastry and roll one way to form a long rectangle. Fold the pastry three times back on itself to form a square again. Repeat once more and chill. Cut the pastry into four even pieces then roll out to make four lids.

FOR THE FILLING

Using a large saucepan, fry the mushrooms and silverskin onions in beef dripping until they have a bit of colour. Add the garlic, carrot, celery and onion then cook for a further 10 minutes. Stir in the tomato purée and herbs. Continue to cook for around 5 minutes.

Toss the diced beef in the flour and seasoning then pan fry separately until nicely browned. Deglaze the pan with the Guinness or stout and beef stock, then transfer the contents to the pan of vegetables and cook the filling on a low heat for about 2 hours, until the meat is tender and falling apart. Place the beef stew into your pie dishes and set aside to cool for 30 minutes.

FOR THE GARNISH

Toss all the ingredients together in a small bowl so everything is dressed with the vinegar.

TO ASSEMBLE

Press the marrow bones into the centre of the stew, gently score a cross in the centre of each pastry rectangle and place the lid onto the pie, allowing the bone to poke through the centre. Crimp the edges of the pastry using your fingers and thumb, then brush the tops with beaten egg.

Place the pies in the oven for 20 minutes until the pastry is golden brown, then serve with the herby salad, pickles, buttered greens and fluffy mashed potato.

Preparation time: 30 minutes | Cooking time: 2 ½ hours | Serves: 4 individual pies

MUSSELS WITH CIDER, LEEKS AND CREAM

This recipe is super easy and makes a beautiful starter. We source our mussels from Fowey in Cornwall. It's best to speak to a trusted fishmonger to ensure your mussels are fresh and from a sustainable source.

1 small leek, sliced

Knob of butter

8 rashers of smoked streaky bacon

4 cloves of garlic, chopped

1kg mussels

250ml cider

250ml double cream

1 lemon, juiced

Small bunch of chives, finely chopped

Salt and pepper

Firstly, sweat the leek in butter until soft and set aside. In a separate large heavy-based pan, fry the bacon until crisp. Add the chopped garlic and softened leeks to the bacon then cook for a further minute. Add the mussels to the pan, add the cider and cover with a lid.

Cook for 3 minutes until the mussels begin to open, then add the cream and simmer gently for a further 2 minutes until all the mussels have opened fully. Discard any mussels that are still closed. Add lemon juice, chives and seasoning to taste.

Serve with some hunks of warm sourdough to mop up the juices!

Preparation time: 10 minutes | Cooking time: 10 minutes | Serves: 4

BANANA CAKE

This is our twist on the nation's favourite dessert, sticky toffee pudding. We substitute
dates for banana and add a shot of cut rum into the molten toffee sauce.

FOR THE CAKE

100g soft unsalted butter

100g sugar

200g self-raising flour

2 eggs

1 tsp vanilla essence

3 bananas, peeled

1 tsp bicarbonate of soda

1 tsp baking powder

FOR THE BANANA PURÉE

3 whole bananas, unpeeled

15g Demerara sugar

5ml vanilla essence

½ lemon, juiced

FOR THE CARAMELISED PECANS

100g pecans

100g caster sugar

1g salt

FOR THE CUT RUM AND TOFFEE SAUCE

150g butter

300g dark muscovado sugar

2 tbsp black treacle

200g double cream

50ml spiced cut rum

TO SERVE

1 fresh banana, sliced

FOR THE CAKE

Cream the butter and sugar together and then add the flour, eggs and vanilla essence. Mix until well combined. Mash the bananas until soft and almost puréed, then fold through the cake mixture. Stir in the bicarbonate of soda and baking powder then transfer the cake mixture into a parchment-lined tin. Cover lightly with foil and cook at 160°c for 25 minutes, then remove the tin foil and cook for a further 10 minutes until golden brown.

Check the cake is cooked by pushing a skewer into the deepest part of the cake; if it comes out clean the cake is done. Place on a wire rack to cool before portioning.

FOR THE BANANA PURÉE

Place the bananas on an ovenproof tray in their skins and cook under a hot grill for 10 minutes. Once soft, and black on the outside, leave the bananas to cool before peeling them and mashing with the remaining ingredients until smooth.

FOR THE CARAMELISED PECANS

Toast the pecans in a dry non-stick frying pan over a medium heat. Once they are brown, add the sugar and salt, continue to heat until caramelised, then transfer to a cold tray and leave to cool.

FOR THE CUT RUM AND TOFFEE SAUCE

Melt the butter, sugar and treacle in a medium-sized pan over a low heat. Once the sugar has dissolved, slowly pour in the cream and then stir in the cut rum.

TO SERVE

Place the portion of warm banana cake into the bowl and spoon over the toffee sauce. Spoon some banana purée around the cake and scatter over some caramelised pecans. Add slices of fresh banana (for an extra detail these can be dipped in sugar and blowtorched until golden) and serve.

Preparation time: 20 minutes | Cooking time: 45 minutes | Serves: 6

NATURALLY INNOVATIVE

PINKMANS IS A PLACE WHERE OLD MEETS NEW. TRADITIONS ARE CHERISHED WHILE NEW IDEAS ARE EXPLORED. AT ITS HEART IS A BAKERY FROM WHICH NATURALLY DELICIOUS FOOD EMERGES EVERY DAY.

Pinkmans is a bakery with a passion for natural ingredients, wild yeast baking and fantastic food to take out or eat in. The upmarket dining hall is centred around its open kitchen, complete with wood-fired oven, from which food emerges onto a copper counter to be served in the convivial surroundings. It might not look like a typical bakery but at the heart of the business are real bakers and lots and lots of baking. Pizzas, fresh bread, sandwiches, cakes and tarts are all on the extensive menus, which people can enjoy all day.

From breakfast to cocktails, Pinkmans aims to be inclusive and modern with a wide range of vegan and gluten free options across their menus and a welcoming attitude to all diners. The bakery was established in 2015 by Steven Whibley, Troels Bendix and Michael Engler, who is still the head baker leading today's team. As sourdough specialists and keen innovators, they have become famed for 'sour-dough-nuts' which is a 'dessert in a doughnut' according to the bakers. Pinkmans also scooped Best Sandwich at the 2018 British Sandwich Awards which the café is well known for.

"The buzz and energy at Pinkmans comes from making and baking everything in the same space as we sell it. In most places where you buy your bread, the bakers are non-existent, being packed off in some production facility that may make things easier but loses the excitement and passion that comes with wild yeast baking. Pinkmans is our attempt to change that."

Pinkmans is hugely supportive of local suppliers, using Bristol-based Buxton Butchers for the meat, flour from Shipton Mill, CackleBean eggs, Freehand for the coffee and a selection of local breweries for the eclectic beer and cider selection.

As sourdough specialists, wild yeast starters are another key ingredient and part of the reason that Pinkmans' breads, pastries and pizzas are so irresistible. Bristolians can now enjoy their favourites at home or in the office thanks to the 'Special Order' catering service that gives customers the option to collect or have their order delivered. Breakfast, lunch, afternoon tea, cakes and breads are all available through the online shop.

With an eye on the past and another on the future, this truly contemporary bakery continues to keep things fresh and interesting with inspired baking the natural way.

PACKAGED BAKERY

GRANOLA 5.50
ESPRESSO 8.50

SPECIAL ORDER
ASK US WHAT WE CAN DO

LARGE CAKE
48 HOURS NOTICE
BESPOKE AVAILABLE

PICNIC 19.50
2 SANDWICHES
1 SALAD BOX
2 CAKES
2 BEVERAGES

pinkmans

V.L.T BREAKFAST SANDWICH

Our Bacon, Spinach & Roast Tomato toasted sandwich is a firm favourite at Pinkmans, but our vegan alternative is giving it a run for its money. The sandwich has the smokiness and juiciness you expect from its meatier cousin and is always recommended by the team here. All the prep can be done days in advance so it's quick to put together for breakfast or a lunch feast. We use white sourdough but any good quality bread will work well.

FOR THE MUSHROOM AUBERGINES

150g button mushrooms

Salt and pepper

1 medium aubergine

FOR THE CRISPY COCONUT

150ml mushroom stock (reserved from aubergines)

75g coconut shavings

FOR THE PIQUILLO PEPPER MAYONNAISE

100g piquillo peppers

125ml soya milk

15ml lemon juice

20g wholegrain mustard

3g fine sea salt

300ml pomace oil

TO FINISH

4 slices of Pinkmans' white sourdough bread

1 medium gem lettuce, washed and chopped

20g sun blushed tomatoes, drained

FOR THE MUSHROOM AUBERGINES

Slice the button mushrooms then place them in a tray. Season with salt and pepper then cover with tin foil and place in a preheated oven at 160°c for 20 minutes or until the juices have been released and the mushrooms are cooked through. Drain off the cooking liquor and keep this as well as the cooked mushrooms.

Slice the aubergines lengthways in ½cm thick slices and lay on a lined baking tray. Brush each slice of aubergine with the reserved mushroom liquor then place in a preheated oven at 200°c for 5 to 8 minutes or until golden in colour.

FOR THE CRISPY COCONUT

Mix the remaining mushroom liquor with the coconut shavings in a bowl. Spread the coconut out on a lined baking tray and place in a preheated oven at 180°c for 5 to 10 minutes or until golden brown and crispy.

FOR THE PIQUILLO PEPPER MAYONNAISE

Using a food processor, purée the piquillo peppers with the soya milk, lemon juice, wholegrain mustard and salt. When the mixture is smooth, slowly start to pour in the pomace oil while the processor is running to emulsify the mayonnaise.

TO FINISH

Toast the four slices of white sourdough bread and warm through the mushroom-flavoured aubergine slices. Spread two slices of toasted sourdough with plenty of piquillo mayo, then layer the chopped lettuce and sun blushed tomatoes onto the prepared slices. Cover with the roasted mushrooms and aubergine slices, then sprinkle with the crispy coconut. Top your V.L.T with the second piece of toasted sourdough and enjoy.

Preparation time: 30 minutes | Cooking time: 30 minutes | Serves: 2

CUSTARD BRIOCHE WITH BLUEBERRIES AND CRÈME FRAÎCHE

This is one of our customers' favourite breakfast dishes at the bakery. We used to use leftover brioche, but it's become so popular we now bake it especially for this dish. You can make the brioche, custard and blueberry compote the day before and put them together quickly for breakfast, brunch or even a pudding. You could soak white sourdough in the custard instead of brioche and cook it in the same way, or omit the blueberries and include crispy bacon drizzled in maple syrup.

FOR THE BRIOCHE

500g strong white flour
70g caster sugar
12g fresh yeast
180ml whole milk
3 large free-range eggs
100g unsalted butter
8g salt
1 egg, beaten

FOR THE CRÈME ANGLAISE

1200ml whole milk
100g honey
1 vanilla pod
225g egg yolk
100g caster sugar
2g salt

FOR THE BLUEBERRY COMPOTE

500g frozen blueberries
150g caster sugar
10ml lemon juice

TO SERVE

Knob of butter
100g crème fraîche

FOR THE BRIOCHE

Combine the flour, caster sugar, fresh yeast, milk, eggs and butter in the bowl of a table top mixer. Using a dough hook, mix slowly until you have a soft elastic dough. Leave it to rest for 10 minutes and then mix in the salt.

Shape the brioche dough into 100g balls and place them in a row in a 20cm by 10cm lined baking tin. Prove somewhere warm until doubled in size (about 1 hour 30 minutes) and the balls have merged to form a loaf.

Glaze the loaf with beaten egg and bake in a preheated oven at 200°c for around 20 minutes, or until golden brown. When the brioche has baked, remove it from the tin and leave to cool.

FOR THE CRÈME ANGLAISE

Combine the milk and honey in a pan, add the vanilla pod and bring to a simmer. In a separate bowl, whisk the egg yolk, caster sugar and salt together. Pour the simmered milk onto the egg yolk mixture and whisk them together. Return the crème anglaise to the pan and cook out on a low heat until it has thickened enough to coat the back of a spoon. Pass through a sieve to remove any lumps and then chill until ready to serve.

FOR THE BLUEBERRY COMPOTE

Combine the blueberries, caster sugar and lemon juice in a pan. Bring to a simmer on a low heat then simmer for 30 minutes, stirring occasionally. Leave the compote to cool if making ahead.

TO SERVE

Slice the brioche loaf into 2cm slices and soak each slice in the cooled crème anglaise for 2 minutes. Fry the custard brioche in a pan on a medium heat with a knob of butter. Turn the slices once so that both sides cook evenly until golden brown. Warm the blueberry compote while cooking the brioche.

Place two slices of custard brioche on each plate, spoon over the warm blueberry compote and finish with a generous dollop of crème fraîche on the side.

Preparation time: 1 hour, plus 1 hour 30 minutes proving | Cooking time: 10 minutes | Serves: 4

GREEN FINGERS

FOCUSING ON ORGANIC METHODS OF PRODUCING FOOD THAT ARE ETHICAL AND ENVIRONMENTALLY POSITIVE, RADFORD MILL IS A FARM AND SHOP RECONNECTING PEOPLE WITH LOCALLY GROWN, SUSTAINABLE PRODUCE.

Radford Mill Farm Shop is an outlet for people to taste the benefits of organic farming, but the land its produce is grown on offers even more ways for people to connect with where their food comes from. The farm, located in the countryside near Bath, has been organic for over 40 years and has always provided the majority of vegetables for the shop in Bristol. The team are now also focusing on building ecosystems on the farm and creating habitats for wild life, which goes hand in hand with selling locally as part of an environmentally friendly model.

A wide variety of fruit, vegetables and salad is grown on the five acres of land at Radford Mill, which has gradually expanded over the years and also has an orchard, a squash field and a recently planted 'forest' of acorn and willow trees which has been designed to protect local wildlife. In addition, some greens such as kale and spinach can be grown all year round in the polytunnels, but the focus is on seasonality. This is encouraged in the shop too, even extending to the juice bar where menus change depending on the ingredients available.

The farm also provides eggs from the free-range chickens who are fed organically, and has recently introduced bees from which the team hope to ethically produce honey for the shop. Wholefoods range from tinned goods to grains and cereals, alongside spices and loose leaf teas. The shop has already reduced single use plastics in the interests of sustainability, and there are plans in place to use refill stations where possible. There are lots of options for those following gluten-free or vegan diets too, and of course an emphasis on home-grown and local ingredients.

If the shop is the first link to natural produce, visiting the farm is the logical next step. Radford Mill has a public walkway open all year round, as well as guided tours and events that mark turning points in the calendar such as the end of the harvest festival. Over the summer, music festivals and plenty of weddings are also held on the land, bringing people into contact with nature and teaching them a little about growing your own food too. A worldwide volunteer scheme known as WWOOF also brings people from all corners of the globe to work on Radford Mill Farm, learning about organic methods and contributing to the venture that provides good food in greener ways.

SUPER GREENS & CANNELLINI BEAN SOUP

A hearty, healthy Italian-inspired vegan soup, packed full of vitamins and great for lifting the spirits on a cold, wintry day. Perfect for using up any hardy, woody herbs in the garden. Recipe by Harry Haynes.

2 tbsp olive oil

2 white onions, chopped

5 cloves of garlic, chopped (keep one whole)

1 large potato, peeled and diced

5 sprigs of thyme, leaves picked and finely chopped

5 sage leaves, finely chopped

Bunch of fresh rosemary, leaves picked and finely chopped

1 litre lower salt vegan stock

1 bunch kale or cavolo nero, stalks removed and leaves chopped

1 bunch of spinach

2 tins of cannellini beans, drained

2 bay leaves

Salt and pepper, to taste

½ a lemon, zested

Heat the oil in a large pan over medium heat. Add the onion, garlic, potato and fresh herbs except for one tablespoon of rosemary. Cook while stirring occasionally until the vegetables start to soften, for about 8 minutes.

Now add the stock, kale and spinach. Bring the soup to a boil, reduce the heat to low-medium and simmer gently until the potatoes are soft, for about 10 minutes. Using a hand blender, blitz the soup three or four times, just enough to thicken it while keeping it a little chunky for texture.

Add the beans and bay leaves and simmer for a further 10 minutes. Add salt and pepper to taste.

For the topping, mince the remaining clove of garlic and combine this with the lemon zest and tablespoon of chopped rosemary. This will bring a real zingy freshness to your hot soup.

Serve the soup with a small sprinkling of the zesty topping and a slice of warm, crusty bread.

Preparation time: 10 minutes | Cooking time: 25 minutes | Serves: 4

A GROWING COMMUNITY

FAMILY-OWNED GREENGROCERS REG THE VEG HAS BEEN PART OF THE INDEPENDENT COMMUNITY IN CLIFTON FOR OVER 40 YEARS, STEADFASTLY SUPPORTING LOCAL GROWERS AND PRODUCERS.

In the heart of Clifton Village, a tiny Georgian building on a pedestrianised street has been home to the same greengrocer's since at least the 1950s. Two decades later, the shop gained its iconic name – Reg the Veg – when it was purchased by Reg Meek, and was taken on by the Hagons in 2009. It's now run by Tom Hagon, along with his partner Beth, mum and dad Julie and John, and brother-in-law Matt, with a small but passionate team of employees. Their aim is to provide continuity and sustainability for both sides of the business, by providing great variety and affordability for customers while supporting the local growers in the area that, sadly, are declining as supermarkets have grown over the decades.

However, at Reg the Veg you will always find a wide range of fresh produce, the majority of which is grown in the region and bought from St Phillips fruit and veg market. Lots of the seasonal vegetables travel no more than a few miles from Failand Farm, for example, and during summer all the strawberries come from the same single producer. Strode Valley Organics, just outside the city, supply mixed leaves and for more exotic options co-owner Tom will scour Bristol's food markets.

"Our way of approaching the sourcing side of the business feels natural to me," he explains. "It needs to be a full circle, with people working together so that we can all protect our livelihoods." Tom also appreciates the community feel that surrounds Reg the Veg not just on their street in Clifton, but within Bristol as the foodie scene has flourished over recent years. It creates a nice atmosphere for customers and visitors discovering the area's many hidden gems.

The business' long history also attracts people, and the family have spoken to shoppers who remember the early days of the shop, even before it was a greengrocer's. Many drop by as part of their daily routine, so there are always familiar faces to be seen and friendly chat to be had. The family-run greengrocer's is also a popular supplier of choice for many restaurants, cafés, pubs and others across Bristol thanks to its fresh local produce and personable ownership.

Proving that the old-fashioned way is sometimes the best, Reg the Veg continues to offer a warm and welcoming place to find quality produce while looking after the wonderful growers that offer a sustainable and more eco-friendly alternatives to supermarkets, allowing shoppers to support the community and the family who are committed to making that possible.

BETH'S TASTY TABBOULEH

*Tabbouleh is a Middle Eastern salad made with bulgur wheat and loads of
fresh herbs. I have always loved it, and have perfected this recipe after years of
experimenting with various ingredients. Reg the Veg is a treasure trove of fresh
and often exotic fruit, vegetables and herbs, so inspiration came easy! I sometimes
add some finely chopped fresh kale leaves to make it extra green, and add some
more texture. We stock all of the ingredients listed throughout the year, and it can
be served alongside a barbecue in the summer or a roast chicken in the winter.*

200g bulgur wheat

4 ripe tomatoes, roughly chopped

I bunch of spring onions, finely sliced

I large bunch of mint, finely chopped

2 large bunches of flat leaf parsley, finely chopped

10 large green olives, sliced

I pomegranate

Handful of walnuts

Good quality olive oil

½ lemon, juiced

Salt and pepper

Cook the bulgur wheat on the hob following the instructions on the packet, then drain and leave to cool.

In a large bowl, combine the tomatoes, spring onions, chopped herbs, olives, and the seeds from the pomegranate.

Gently toast the walnuts in a dry pan, then chop them roughly and add to the bowl, along with the cooled bulgur wheat.

Dress the tabbouleh with a generous glug of olive oil, lemon juice and salt and pepper.

Preparation time: 10 minutes | Cooking time: 10-15 minutes | Serves: 6

BUON APPETITO

OPEN FOR BREAKFAST, BRUNCH, LUNCH, APERITIVO AND DINNER, ROSEMARINO IS A LITTLE GEM TO ENJOY ANYTIME, WHETHER THAT'S FOR A FULL ITALIAN FEAST OR SIMPLY A COFFEE WHILE READING THE PAPERS.

Tony de Brito, Sam Fryer and Mirco Bertoldi met working in the food and drink industry. In 2010 their shared vision for an Italian restaurant became a reality, and Rosemarino was established. The eatery combines casual Italian dining with renowned all-day brunches that have gained a real following in the city. For many people, in fact, Rosemarino is synonymous with a good breakfast! Every year since 2012 the restaurant has scooped awards from Bristol Good Food including 'Best Italian' and 'Best Breakfast' as well as 'Best Front of House'.

The success of this venture is down to a winning combination of the relaxed atmosphere and a dynamic menu. Rather than being restricted to starters, then mains, then desserts, dinner at Rosemarino is organised into cichetti – including olives, arancini and bruschetta – alongside antipasti which can be shared or not, pasta dishes and dolci (sweet options that include affogato, formaggio or cheese boards and gelato).

"The emphasis is on freshly prepared food using a range of locally based suppliers and producers, no fancy or complicated masterpieces – just great food from great ingredients. Our lunch and dinner menus are based on satisfying regional Italian specialities and change weekly allowing us to make the most of seasonal ingredients when they're at their best," say Mirco, Sam and Tony.

Mirco's heritage comes through in these specialities, even using his dad's home-cured speck which is sent especially from Trentino, and in the dishes that are made to family recipes and have been passed down the generations. Homemade focaccia is baked fresh every morning and ingredients are sourced from friends of Rosemarino in the area, including Attic Tea and Clifton Coffee.

The restaurant's drinks offering is complemented by a 'small but quirky' wine list featuring options from small producers creating interesting alternatives to generic Pinot Grigio or Chianti. Rosemarino's founders believe that wines should have a sense of place and express the balance between vineyard, climate and grape. The list changes seasonally to reflect this ethos, and many of the wines are made using organic and bio-dynamic principles.

From supporting local businesses to making the most of its Italian roots, Rosemarino continues to provide Bristol with beautifully made food in warm and welcoming surroundings, and is the perfect place for an after-work drink and a nibble or a spot of indulgence amidst true Italian hospitality.

SEAFOOD SAFFRON FREGOLA

Fregola, which means 'crumbs' in the dialect, is a famous type of pasta from Sardinia, made with semolina flour and water. The dough is passed through a colander to create pasta similar in appearance to Israeli giant couscous, once dried the pasta is slowly oven toasted. It can be cooked like risotto rice and flavours can be varied by adding different stocks.

Fregola goes very well with any kind of fish, and in the coastal areas of Sardinia it normally makes up the starch element of a punchy seafood stew. Its origins can be traced back to the Middle East and our decadent recipe pays homage to this with the addition of saffron. We love this ingredient because for us it is a symbol of the melting pot of cultures which go into Italian cuisine.

60ml extra-virgin olive oil

1 red onion, finely chopped

2 cloves of garlic

400g fregola

65ml white wine

500ml fish stock

250g mussels

250g clams

8 king prawns, shelled

1g saffron filaments

30g butter

80g dill, finely chopped

In a medium-size pot, heat half of the olive oil and add the finely chopped red onion and one clove of garlic. Add the fregola and let it toast for at least 2 minutes. Then add half of the wine, let it evaporate and gradually add fish stock until the fregola is nicely cooked and al dente (firm).

5 minutes before the fregola is cooked, heat the rest of the olive oil in a different pan then add the other clove of garlic, mussels, clams and the rest of white wine. Cover with a lid until the mussels and clams are open, then add the prawns, saffron, butter and dill. Let it cook for another 2 minutes or until the prawns are cooked.

Transfer the seafood with the juices gently into the fregola mixture and cook for 1 more minute to bind all the ingredients together.

Serve with a drizzle of olive oil, fresh dill leaves and lemon zest.

Preparation time: 10 minutes | Cooking time: approx. 20 minutes | Serves: 4

EVERYTHING YOU WANT
FOR THE
WEEKEND

THIS BRISTOL-BASED BAR AND CAFÉ COMBINES GREAT FOOD WITH THE FLOW OF LOCAL BEER AND AN ATMOSPHERE THAT LIVES UP TO ITS NAME.

Since 2010, The Social Bar & Café has provided a warm and intimate haven right in the heart of Bristol. Customers have come to rely on its allure of hearty food, a well-stocked bar and live music throughout the year. After entering a partnership with the previous owner, Chris, in June 2019, Charlie, Georgia and Curtis – also the head chef – pledged to keep things moving in the same direction. With the help of Chris, who set up the venue initially, they are sticking to The Social's ethos but expanding its offering.

Using locally-sourced ingredients, for instance, is important to all of them. The menus have been fine-tuned with simplified dishes across the board, from all-day breakfasts to tapas. Comforting pub lunches influence the food, which is always made from scratch with an eye for quality produce. Sharing plates and burgers are some of the tried and tested favourites, with the reassurance that produce is knowledgably sourced from butchers and suppliers around Bristol.

When The Social transforms into bar mode, dusk brings with it a warming selection of tapas that changes daily. It's perfect finger-food shared over a glass or two of local gin or your favourite tipple. With a keg line and an ever-changing bottle selection – which includes many from Bristol breweries – plus cocktails and a generous collection of spirits, there's plenty to choose from. The marriage between café and bar truly comes into its own at the weekend; since the new owners introduced live music sessions and DJs to the events calendar, revellers can enjoy food, drink and entertainment all in one cosy venue.

If you want to take a break from the buzz of a Saturday evening at The Social, the recently refurbished beer garden is there to welcome you with a dose of fresh air. Since the outdoor space is under cover and has plenty of heaters, it can be used all year round. Looking to the future, the team plan to make their café and bar even more eco-friendly. They are already participants of a refill water bottle scheme, are eliminating single-use plastics from the venue, and offer a variety of vegan options on the menu. Social by name and social by nature, it's a place for anyone, any time!

GLAMORGAN SAUSAGE

*Glamorgan sausages have been part of our menu since pretty much the beginning.
They are a customer favourite as part of our veggie breakfast, or in a sandwich.
The way the outside crisps up and the cheese goes melty in the middle is delicious
and doubly naughty. Enjoy!*

250g breadcrumbs

2 leeks (about 400g)

50g unsalted butter

200g mature cheddar

50g parsley

2 tbsp wholegrain Dijon mustard

1 tbsp cracked black pepper

1 egg

Vegetable oil

To make your own breadcrumbs, dry out several slices of bread in an oven at a low temperature and then break up and transfer into a food processer until all the big bits have broken down.

Trim the leeks slightly but leave the nice green tops on, give them a wash and then chop them as finely as possible.

Heat up the butter in a frying pan and fry the leeks until soft, then leave to cool. Grate the cheddar into a bowl, then finely chop the parsley and add it to bowl with cheese. Add the breadcrumbs, mustard and black pepper then crack the whole egg.

When the leeks are cool, add them to the bowl and – with a pair of gloves on – use your hands to combine everything as thoroughly as possible. If the mixture isn't holding together, you may need to add another egg or more breadcrumbs. Roll the mixture into even-sized sausage shapes.

Heat up a deep fat fryer to 180°c and fry the sausages until the cheese in the middle has melted and they are golden in colour. If you don't have a fryer, you can shallow fry the sausages in vegetable oil.

Preparation time: 30 minutes | Cooking time: 2 minutes | Serves: 10

ALL HANDS ON DECK

BRISTOL'S FLOATING TAPAS RESTAURANT TAKES YOU ON A TRIP AROUND THE MEDITERRANEAN VIA ELEGANT COCKTAILS AND DISHES FULL OF FLAVOUR, ALL WITHOUT LEAVING THE CITY HARBOUR.

Under the Stars was established by Andrew and Leah Meehill back in 2010, starting life as a bar but becoming a food-focused destination over the years. The floating restaurant is moored in Bristol Harbour, boasting a large open deck above an indoor floor for the perfect atmosphere whatever the weather. In 2017 Andrew and Leah were able to purchase the boat and complete a full refurbishment, making it their own with a few subtle nods to the nautical nature of the venue, a classic and contemporary drinks selection and a menu that takes travel as its starting point.

Since there is plenty of crossover when it comes to Mediterranean food, Under the Stars doesn't restrict diners to only Spanish tapas. The small plates and sharing dishes take in all the complementary flavours out there – passing through Greece, Turkey, Morocco, France and Italy to name just a few – alongside a selection of stone-baked pizzas which are also made in-house within the kitchen in the boat's hold. Around half the menu is vegetarian and there are always vegan options available too, fitting for the social side of tapas-style dining which welcomes everyone.

Under the Stars encourages an informal atmosphere which suits the casual yet exciting food and drink. It's a popular spot for dinner dates, where people can order more as and when while trying and sharing a variety of dishes, without getting food envy! The family-run restaurant also welcomes groups of up to 20 people. When the sun shines, al fresco eating is always on the menu thanks to an open top deck, but the candlelight and harbour views through large windows downstairs make for an equally special evening out.

The couple enjoy freedom to make their food accessible but imaginative, drawing on influences and the availability of local produce to update the menus. For returning customers – of which there are many – this means that Under the Stars always has something new to try alongside enduring favourites. Like the dishes, the venue itself is always evolving, so the team at Under the Stars are looking forward to continuing their improvements year on year and creating unique experiences on Bristol's waterfront.

SPICED CAULIFLOWER WITH CELERIAC PURÉE

We pair our roasted spiced cauliflower with celeriac, the unsung hero of the vegetable world. Our smooth celeriac purée has a sweet earthy flavour and is complemented perfectly by the crunchy parsnip crisps and truffle oil. This dish is perfect for those cold winter evenings and is a firm favourite on our seasonal menu.

FOR THE SPICED CAULIFLOWER

1 large cauliflower, trimmed

1 tsp ground cumin

1 tsp ground coriander

1 tsp ground turmeric

1 tsp smoked paprika

Sea salt and black pepper

1 tbsp olive oil

FOR THE CELERIAC PURÉE

50ml olive oil

1 large onion, peeled and chopped

2 cloves of garlic, peeled and sliced

2 bay leaves

1 celeriac, peeled and diced (the smaller you cut it the quicker it will cook)

500ml vegetable stock

2 tbsp tahini

½ tsp ground cumin

½ tsp ground coriander

½ tsp smoked paprika

Sea salt and black pepper

1 lemon, juiced

FOR THE PARSNIP CRISPS

50-100ml vegetable oil

1 parsnip, peeled and shaved

TO SERVE

Truffle oil

Fresh parsley

Black onion seeds

FOR THE SPICED CAULIFLOWER

Cut the cauliflower florets into even sizes, slicing into halves or quarters where necessary. Put them into a baking tray and coat evenly with all the spices and olive oil. Cover your tray with foil and roast in the oven at 200°c for 30 minutes, removing the foil for the final 10 minutes of cooking.

FOR THE CELERIAC PURÉE

Put a healthy glug of olive oil in a large saucepan and fry the onion until soft. Add the garlic and bay leaves with the diced celeriac. Fry for 5 to 8 minutes, keeping everything moving to make sure nothing burns. Pour in the stock and simmer for 15 minutes until the celeriac is soft. Remove the pan from the heat, discard the bay leaves and transfer everything to your food processor. Add the tahini, spices and seasoning to the mixture with a squeeze of lemon juice then blend until smooth.

FOR THE PARSNIP CRISPS

Pour roughly 1cm of oil into a small frying pan. Put the pan over a medium heat and bring the oil up to temperature. Fry the parsnip shavings until they start to turn golden, then remove them from the pan and place onto kitchen roll to absorb any excess oil. Alternatively, the parsnip crisps can be cooked in the oven if you feel more comfortable with that process.

TO SERVE

Divide the celeriac purée between six tapas plates and spread it evenly. Place the spiced cauliflower on top with a few parsnip crisps and then finish with truffle oil, fresh parsley and black onion seeds.

Preparation time: 10 minutes | Cooking time: 30 minutes | Serves: 6

DIRECTORY

THESE GREAT BUSINESSES HAVE SUPPORTED THE MAKING OF THIS BOOK;
PLEASE SUPPORT AND ENJOY THEM.

1766 BAR & KITCHEN

Bristol Old Vic
King Street
Bristol BS1 4ED
Telephone: 0117 907 2682
Website: www.bristololdvic.org.uk/food-drink
*Inspiring all day dining in Bristol Old Vic's multi-award-winning
foyer.*

BATH CULTURE HOUSE

Unit 1
The Old Saw Mill
Ubley
Bristol BS40 6PE
Telephone: 07876 758588
Website: www.bathculturehouse.com
*Fabulously fermented artisan vegan food and drink, handmade
and cultured in Somerset.*

THE BATH SOFT CHEESE COMPANY

Park Farm
Kelston
Bath BA1 9AQ
Telephone: 01225 331601
Website: parkfarm.co.uk
*Award-winning organic cheese made by hand at Park Farm,
Kelston near Bath with milk from our own cows.*

THE BRISTOL FOOD TOUR

Email: thebristolfoodtour@gmail.com
Website: www.thebristolfoodtour.com
Instagram: @thebristolfoodtour
Twitter: @bristolfoodtour
Facebook: www.facebook.com/thebristolfoodtour

BRACE & BROWNS

43 Whiteladies Road
Bristol BS8 2LS
Telephone: 0117 973 7800
Website: www.braceandbrowns.co.uk
*A warm and welcoming bar and restaurant with beautifully
curated small plates, an emphasis on local produce, and a wide
variety of delicious cocktails.*

BURGER THEORY

37-38 St Stephen's Street
Bristol BS1 1JX
Telephone: 0117 929 7818
Website: burgertheory.co.uk
*Creative food and drink including burgers, cocktails, dirty fries,
craft beers and epic cheesecakes.*

CASTLE FARM MIDFORD

Castle Farm
Midford
Bath
Somerset BA2 7PU
Telephone: 07564 783307
Website: www.castlefarmmidford.co.uk
*A unique restaurant offering an array of cuisines and dining
experiences, set on an organic farm in the rolling hills of Midford,
just south of Bath in Somerset.*

THE CHOCOLATE TART

The Old Malthouse
Kent Road
Congresbury
Bristol BS49 5BD
Telephone: 01934 876881
Website: www.thechocolatetart.co.uk
Professional chocolatier's kitchen teaching all things chocolate and more. Come on your own or as part of a group, gift a food lover a voucher, and stay in the double ensuite accommodation.

CHEW VALLEY WEDDINGS

Woodford Lane
Chew Stoke
Bristol BS40 8XR
Website: www.chewvalleyweddings.co.uk
Event venue space overlooking Chew Valley Lake.

THE COMMUNITY FARM

Denny Lane
Chew Magna BS40 8SZ
Telephone: 01275 295029
Website: www.thecommunityfarm.co.uk
A nature-friendly farm, growing and selling organic produce via a local veg box scheme and outlets, with profits being put back into the community.

EAT DRINK EVENTS LTD

Yurt Lush
Clock Tower Yard
Bristol BS1 6QH
Website: www.eatdrinkbristolfashion.co.uk
Sustainable food in interesting spaces.

THE FISH SHOP

143 Gloucester Road
Bristol BS7 8BA

THE FISH SHOP

2 Third Avenue
Bath BA2 3NY
Telephone: 0117 924 1988
Website: www.lovethefishshop.co.uk
Specialising in really fresh dayboat fish and seafood from the south coast, with shops in Bath and Bristol stocking a wide range of shellfish, smoked fish, deli products, sauces and frozen seafood.

FOSTERS EVENTS

Unit 5 Avonside Road
Feeder Road
Bristol BS2 0UQ
Telephone: 0117 977 6611
Website: www.fostersevents.co.uk
Exceptional events and culinary creativeness from the south-west's leading caterer.

GOOD SIXTY LTD

1 Temple Way
Bristol BS2 0BY
Telephone: 0117 230 5660
Website: www.goodsixty.co.uk
Artisan food and drink from the very best local independents in Bristol and Bath, delivered to your door by eco-friendly bike!

GRAPE & GRIND

101 Gloucester Road
Bristol BS7 8AT
Telephone: 0117 924 8718
Website: www.grapeandgrind.co.uk
Award-winning shop on Bristol's bustling Gloucester Road, offering a hand-picked selection of wines, local craft beers, international spirits and coffee.

HARTLEY FARM SHOP & KITCHEN

Winsley
Bradford on Avon
Wiltshire BA15 2JB
Telephone: 01225 864948
Website: www.hartley-farm.co.uk
Email: hello@hartley-farm.co.uk
Family-run ventures on the outskirts of the Cotswolds with award-winning farm shops, butchers and farm kitchens serving breakfast and lunch from a delicious seasonal menu seven days a week.

JAMAICA STREET STORES

37-39 Jamaica Street
Bristol BS8 JP
Telephone: 0117 924 9294
Website: www.jamaicastreetstores.com
Family run, sustainably focused, modern British bistro housed in a beautifully refurbished 19th century carriageworks.

JOE'S BAKERY

24 Gloucester Rd
Bishopston
Telephone: 0117 907 1852

JOE'S BAKERY

45 Gloucester Rd
Bishopston
Telephone: 0117 330 3798
Website: www.joesbakery.co.uk
Long-established bakery shop making a wide range of high-quality traditional and sourdough breads, pastries, savouries and sandwiches for the home or on-the-go.

THE LAZY DOG

112 Ashley Down Road
Bristol BS7 9JR
Telephone: 0117 924 4809
Email: info@thelazydogbristol.com
Independently owned community pub with a large beer garden and an emphasis on quality food and drinks.

THE MALL DELI

14 The Mall
Bristol BS8 4DR
Telephone: 0117 973 4440
Website: www.themalldeli.co.uk
Traditional deli and café in Clifton Village bringing great produce from small local suppliers and their own deli kitchen together to eat in or take away.

MARK'S BREAD

291 North Street
Ashton BS3 1JP
Bakery: 07910 979384
Café: 0117 953 7997
Website: www.marksbread.co.uk
Email: info@marksbread.co.uk
Community-friendly bakery, café and shop that creates, bakes and sells delicious food six days a week, specialising in sourdough, traditional yeasted and continental breads.

MEATBOX

Unit 24 Cargo 2
Museum Street
Bristol BS1 6ZA
Website: www.meatboxbristol.co.uk
Ethical 100% pasture fed meat for Bristol.

NESTON FARM SHOP & KITCHEN

Bath Road, Atworth
Melksham
Wiltshire
SN12 8HP
Telephone: 01225 700881
Website: www.nestonfarmshop.co.uk
Email: hello@nestonfarmshop.co.uk
Family-run ventures on the outskirts of the Cotswolds with award-winning farm shops, butchers and farm kitchens serving breakfast and lunch from a delicious seasonal menu seven days a week.

NUTCESSITY

Telephone: 07813 388851
Website: www.nutcessity.co.uk
*Find us on Facebook and Instagram @nutcessity
Premium organic nut butters made with nuts, seeds and coconut, and blended with whole fruit. No peanuts anywhere!*

PASTURE RESTAURANT

2 Portwall Lane
Bristol BS1 6NB
Telephone: 07741 193445
Pasture is about fine dining for everyone, with slick, engaging service, top-quality food and a team whose knowledge is as strong as its passion.

PINKMANS

85 Park Street
Bristol BS1 5PJ
Telephone: 0117 403 2040
Website: www.pinkmans.co.uk
Independent modern bakery café, open all day and specialising in wild yeast baking and sourdough. Home of the sour-dough-nut.

RADFORD MILL FARM

Timsbury
BA2 0QF
Telephone: 01761 479391

RADFORD MILL FARM SHOP

41 Picton Street
Montpelier
Bristol
BS6 5PZ
Telephone: 0117 942 6644
Website: www.radfordmillfarm.com
Organic produce sold in Bristol from a sustainable and environmental friendly farm, which is open to visitors for walks, guided tours and events year-round.

REG THE VEG

6 Boyces Avenue
Clifton
Bristol BS8 4AA
Telephone : 0117 970 6777
Website: www.regtheveg.co.uk
Independent family-run greengrocers in the heart of Clifton Village, proudly providing Bristol with quality fruit and veg for over 50 years.

ROOT

Unit 9 Cargo 1
Gaol Ferry Steps
Bristol BS1 6WP
Website: www.eatdrinkbristolfashion.co.uk
Sustainable food in interesting spaces.

ROSEMARINO

1 York Place
Clifton
Bristol BS8 1AH
Telephone: 0117 973 6677
Website: www.rosemarino.co.uk
Open for breakfast, brunch and lunch with aperitivo and dinner, Rosemarino is a little gem to enjoy anytime, whether it's for a full Italian feast or a coffee while reading the paper.

THE SOCIAL BAR & CAFÉ

130 Cheltenham Road
Stokes Croft
Bristol BS6 5RW
Telephone: 0117 924 4500
Website: thesocialbristol.co.uk
One of Stokes Croft's most popular places to eat, drink and be social! Fresh, locally-sourced food served by friendly staff in a relaxed atmosphere.

THE STORY GROUP LTD

High Street
Blagdon
Bristol BS40 7TA
Website: www.storybutchers.co.uk
Online and local butchers delivering to the Chew Valley from field to fork.

TIPI EVENTS

Herons Green Farm
Compton Martin
Bristol BS40 6NL
Website: www.tipievents.co.uk
Green events in alternative tents.

UNDER THE STARS

Narrow Quay
Harbourside
Bristol BS1 4QA
Telephone: 0117 929 8392
Website: www.underthestarsbar.co.uk
Floating bar and kitchen serving Mediterranean tapas, stone-baked pizzas and a wide variety of cocktails.

VALLEY FEST LTD

Herons Green Farm
Compton Martin
Bristol BS40 6NL
Website: www.valleyfest.co.uk
The best tasting music festival in the South West.

OTHER TITLES AVAILABLE

The Little Book of Cakes & Bakes

Featuring recipes and stories from the kitchens of some of the nation's best bakers and cake-makers.
9781910863480

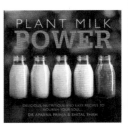

Plant Milk Power

How to create your own delicious, nutritious and nourishing moo-free milks and smoothies.
9781910863411

Tasty & Healthy

Eating well with lactose intolerance, coeliac disease, Crohn's disease, ulcerative colitis and irritable bowel syndrome.
9781910863367

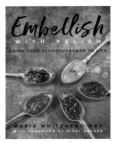

Embellish with Relish

Bring your store cupboard essentials to life with The Hawkshead Relish Cook Book. From hearty hotpots to aromatic curries, these are simple but satisfying meals packed full of flavour. 9781910863497

Sweet Chilli Friday

Simple vegetarian recipes from our kitchen to yours.
9781910863381

RECENT TITLES FROM OUR 'GET STUCK IN' SERIES

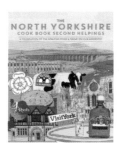

The North Yorkshire Cook Book Second Helpings features Michelin-starred chef Tommy Banks, Shaun Rankin from Grantley Hall, plastic-free shop The Bishy Weigh, as well as distillery, Spirit of Yorkshire. 9781910863565

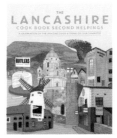

Lancashire Second Helpings Features acclaimed-Lancastrian Steve Smith from the Freemasons at Wiswell, local favourite The Cartford Inn, award-winning Cuckoo Gin and events from Visit Lancashire.
9781910863510

The Cornish Cook Book Featuring Gylly Beach, winner of 'Best Café' in the Southwest 2018, The Rising Sun, Cornwall Life's Pub of the Year and Edie's Kitchen run by Nigel Brown.
978-1-910863-47-3

The Edinburgh and East Coast Cook Book features Masterchef winner Jamie Scott at The Newport, Fhior, Pickering's Gin, Pie Not, Stockbridge Market and much more.
978-1-910863-45-9

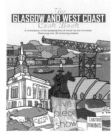

The Glasgow and West Coast Cook Book features The Gannet, Two Fat Ladies, The Spanish Butcher, Hutchesons City Grill, Gamba and much more.
978-1-910863-43-5

The Bristol Cook Book features Dean Edwards, Lido, Clifton Sausage, The Ox, and wines from Corks of Cotham plus lots more.
978-1-910863-14-5

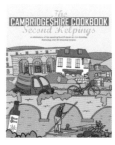

The Cambridgeshire Cook Book: Second Helpings features Mark Abbott of Midsummer House, The Olive Grove, Elder Street Café and much more.
978-1-910863-33-6

The Manchester Cook Book: Second Helpings features Ben Mounsey of Grafene, Hatch, Refuge, Masons, Old School BBQ Bus and much more.
978-1-910863-44-2

The Bath Cook Book features more than 40 recipes from The Chequers, Hare & Hounds, The Beaufort and Blue Quails Deli plus much more.
9781910863176

The Derbyshire Cook Book: Second Helpings features Chris Mapp at The Tickled Trout, Chatsworth Farm Shop, Michelin-starred Fischer's, Peacock and much more.
978-1-910863-34-3

All our books are available from Waterstones, Amazon and good independent bookshops.
FIND OUT MORE ABOUT US AT WWW.MEZEPUBLISHING.CO.UK